MISTAKES ARE MADE FOR *a reason*

TONYA "KANDIE" THOMAS

IBG Publications, Inc.

TONYA "KANDIE" THOMAS

Published by I.B.G. Publications, Inc., a Power to Wealth Company

Web Address: WWW.IBGPublications.Com

admin@IBGPublications.Com / 904-419-9810

Copyright, 2023 by Tonya Thomas

IBG Publications, Inc., Jacksonville, FL

ISBN: 978-1-956266-47-4

Thomas, Tonya
Mistakes Are Made For A Reason

Printed in the United States of America.

Dedication

First and foremost, I would like to thank God for abiding in me and giving me the fortitude to withstand persecution. Please brace yourself and enjoy this reading as I respectively testify about how God delivered me from the dark pits of hell.

Some of the names have been changed to protect the privacy of those involved. The details are true, and my emotions are raw. Although I have always had a desire to share my story, it was in hope of rescuing someone in need and more so at-risk teen girls.

I want you to know this: you matter. It's not by MISTAKE that you are reading my book. It is by divine intention to activate your faith and empower you. Although I allowed myself to be victimized for far too long, my **ONLY REGRET IS NOT ALERTING THE AUTHORITIES!!!**

I encourage you to pick up your head, let go of your past, and use your voice. The life you choose is your choice.

"Therefore confess your sins to each other and pray for each other so that you may be healed...The prayer of the righteous person is powerful and effective."

~James 5:16 (NIV)

My Journey

Although liberating, writing this book has been by far the hardest task I have accomplished. I learned through the process that vulnerability has been my strength.

As I began to acknowledge what transpired, I cried, attempting to make sense of, "How come?" and "Why?" I tried to justify the reasons why my dignity was broken to the core. I knew I couldn't take any more.

I HAD TO BE INTENTIONAL.

"Be mindful: your emotions are formed long before you realize."

~Tonya "Kandie' Thomas

TONYA "KANDIE" THOMAS

MISTAKES ARE MADE FOR *a reason*

TABLE OF CONTENTS

CHAPTER 7:

Acknowledgments

I would like to give a special thank you to my 'village' for their unconditional love throughout my journey: my grandmother, my "Mua" and my Queen, the late Ruby Lee Allen-Graves. She is the most influential person I have ever met.

With your amazing grace, you exemplified what true love is. You were always there to love, nurture and affirm me. *Your talks were not in vain.*

You reassured me God doesn't make mistakes and you would say, "I may not live to witness it, but God will make a way…. um mark my word!"

Granny, I will forever be in debt to you for speaking

life into my dead situation. I can now say, "GRANNY I DID IT!"

To my loving aunt, friend, and confidant Alberta Cummings, the 'Diva of all Divas.' You model what integrity is, and you have been my anchor and a mother figure.

When I was sick, you were there. When I needed my mom, you were there, and you never missed my birthday. I even got a crisp $2 bill this year for my birthday. LOL!

You have always shown me real motherly love and filled the void when I needed it the most. I can't thank you enough.

MISTAKES ARE MADE FOR *a reason*

To my Aunt Ellen (RIP) and Aunt Johnnie Mae who always encouraged me that I was not a mistake. They would always say, "Kandie you are stronger than you realize."

To my uncles, I am grateful for all your TOUGH love and support along my journey. Each of you has impacted my life.

Having you all in my life has been rewarding in many ways. I have watched each of you exemplify what a man, brother, uncle, father, and husband entails.

A special shout out to Uncle Clean (RIP) for always encouraging me to be the "Change I desired to see." Those words have catapulted me until this day.

A special thank you to all (their wives) my aunts, who always had time for me. I will always hold your motherly love and acts of kindness close to my heart that each of you have shown me from childhood.

My loving daughter Te'Onna. I am grateful beyond

words to experience genuine love. I adore the mother and daughter bond we share. I more so thank God for answering my prayers: a healthy child who I can reap the benefits that reciprocated love has to offer.

My sweet, and compassionate granddaughter Ty'Teonna for being wiser than her years. Your uniqueness and creative thinking pushed me when things looked bleak. You were my light at the end of a very dark tunnel.

A special thank you goes out to Leon Jordan my **dearest** friend and **brother**. For stepping up when I

 needed a brother or sibling. You opened your heart, home and arms and you were God sent. True friendship lasts a lifetime. *I love you Lil Bro*

I thank you God for placing these mighty and awesome people in my life. I am beyond thankful because each of you propelled me in your own special way.

Grateful 🖤

Tonya Be Bless

TONYA "KANDIE" THOMAS

Remembering Ruby

'A Tribute To The Matriarch'

I would like to dedicate this book to my grandmother, The late Ruby Lee Allen-Graves.

Your love gave me hope, which increased my faith. You had a heart of gold; your love was authentic, and one of a kind. You were loving, caring and tentative.

It was a joy to be able to give you flowers during my visits to Sacramento, California or during our daily phone calls. I never missed the opportunity to tell or show you how much I loved and appreciated you.

There was nothing you would not do for your grandchildren and you were an important part of my life from my birth until God called you home; I never imagined life without you. Not a day goes by that I don't think about you. However, since losing you I have experienced the meaning of grief.

TONYA "KANDIE" THOMAS

The essence of your love pushed me, and I thank you for all the gifts, love, wisdom, and precious memories.

INTEGRITY, INTEGRITY: THAT'S ME...

Dignity and tenacity define who I am.

Women and men alike are amazed by my strength…

Some are misled by the gray in my head and the blue on my lips.

Diva that's Me…

My presence captivates the room as if it was the ten o'clock news.

The glare from my sexy brown eyes makes them stare.

The lust in their eyes diverts their trust.

The sound of my lovely voice gives them no choice.

Women view me as an illusion …

But to know me is to love me.

My moral compass sets me apart from the rest.

DIVINE INTEGRITY THAT'S ME.

TONYA "KANDIE" THOMAS

Message to my parents and siblings.

I have extended the olive branch several times.

Needless to say, this is not the case.

I want each of you to know I am in a better place.

My life has propelled and I have exhaled as I accepted the hand I was dealt.

Blessings always!!

"When you have given your all, "Chin Up."

TY'TEONNA "TT" KNOWLTON

CHAPTER 1:

Intentional

"Youngstown, Ohio is a midsize city nestled in the northeast part of the state. Located sixty-five miles southeast of Cleveland, and sixty-one miles from Pennsylvania. It has a humid continental climate with cold winters and warm summers. The area is prone to lake-effect snow from nearby Lake Erie during the winter months."

Youngstown is known for being a cultural and historical hub and a center for entertainment and innovation.

It is the ninth largest city, with a population of nearly 70,000. The city was once the capital of steel production in the world.

However, in the 1970s the recession hit and the industry began to decline tremendously. The steel mills were laying off at an alarming pace as the city went bankrupt and crime began to permeate."

My Humble Beginning

This is where my journey began. Mom and Mr. Husband (RIP) were young, happy and in love. They were looking forward to having a large family. He was a few years older and used it to his advantage. Needless to say, that was his plan.

He was a truck driver for The Youngstown Barrel & Drum Co. He worked hard to provide for his family, making decent money.

He controlled the house with an iron fist and a fiery tongue. He did the cooking, budgeting, and grocery shopping. Mom was a young, timid uneducated homemaker who stayed barefoot and pregnant. That was his way of controlling her.

"Controlling is where one partner dominates the other in an unhealthy, self-serving manner."

"It can be difficult to identify controlling behavior when you're in a relationship. It's easy to justify controlling behavior as a sign of caring or love for you. More so, it is important to remember that controlling behavior is not love. It is about power and manipulation."

"People who try to control your movement, decisions or beliefs are more concerned about what they want, than what is best for you."

They had four boys: Basil, Donald (RIP), Biker and Blaze. Several years earlier they lost a daughter and son. The loss of their children left them traumatized.

They often talked about the demise of their late children. Losing their daughter appeared to be more devastating (their only girl) since there was no known cause of death and they wanted a girl. Their son passed from crib death.

"Crib death is an unexpected death of a healthy child younger than one year old, usually during sleep. The cause is not known."

"After losing a child, parents may find themselves experiencing shock denial, anger, depression, hopelessness, guilt, isolation, disorganized thoughts, feelings of acceptance and or a host of other possible thoughts and feelings."

"Without coordination, your marriage will face conflict and tension and you will find yourself working against each other. Good communication is essential for a happy and fulfilling relationship."

The loss caused a lot of tension and pain in their marriage. Not knowing how to channel their pain made life difficult. Never considering counseling was a major issue.

"You have to do the work. —*Iyanla Vanzant*

"Marriage takes work, commitment, and love, but they also needed respect to truly be happy and successful. A marriage based on love and respect doesn't just happen. Both spouses must do their part."

Neither of them took the time to heal. Having done their work, they would have been able to move forward knowing the death of their children had nothing to do with them.

God is in control of life and death; He is intentional.

***

Mr. Husband started keeping odd work hours and when he came home it was obvious, he had been drinking. He would be combative and overbearing.

Mom was feeling overwhelmed with her four rambunctious boys and her wifely duties. As they were pressing through the pain from the loss of their children, their marriage was falling through the cracks. No one took the initiative to address the issue or issues. Not long after they were like two ships in the night.

The boys were getting big and growing fast. I surmise they were aware of the disconnect since the tension was so thick you could cut it with a knife; their communication had crumbled to pieces.

Mentally, Mr. Husband had checked out. He would be gone when the boys woke up and they would be asleep when he came home, leaving all the responsibilities to mom. They both displayed a level of guilt that neither of them was responsible for.

When your marriage is in a downward spiral, you must take time to reevaluate it. You should 'respect' each other's qualities, thoughts, dreams, and capabilities, which means you accept and admire each other's differences.

Their focus was on having a baby girl as if it was going to relieve the pain and get their marriage back on track.

"Emotional healing teaches us life lessons on coping and adjustment. It creates awareness and helps us express our feelings in a proper way."

As they proceeded forward with their dysfunctional life, thirteen months later, God granted their wish for a daughter. She was their 'lil' princess.' They even named her Princess.

They adored everything about her. Everything she did was 'cute' in their eyes. She brought temporary joy to their marriage, but several months later, the marriage took a turn for the worse.

After the many years of abuse, Mom mustered up enough strength to stand up for herself and the children. They agreed to separate, so Mom packed up and moved with her five babies ages newborn to seven years old.

The separation was a joke.

It was a blessing to have "Mua" (RIP) live nearby. She was loving, caring and compassionate; she was like a breath of fresh air. She was a pillar in the community and was known for always helping anyone in need.

Fast forward... Mom, and Mr. Husband both embraced their freedom with no regrets. They enjoyed being separated and acted like parentless, single people. They took the liberty to do as they pleased which consisted of not honoring their marital vows, neglecting their children and partying. They carried on as if they had no responsibilities. They did not realize the 'roles' of a mother and father are important to a child. Mothers provide emotional stability, while fathers provide security and certainty in their lives.

"Mothers are the first indication of the sovereignty of God in our lives. Mothers teach us to have confidence and belief in ourselves. Mothers know from experience how important it is for their children to believe in themselves in order for children to be whole, strong and grow with a healthy estimation of oneself."

***

Mr. Husband's controlling and abusive behavior continued with his impromptu visits. He would show up all hours of the day and night drunk and disrespecting Mom in front of their children with his loud and intimidating voice.

It was apparent the separation was not the solution since they never stopped seeing each other sexually. Showing concern about what the other was doing was evidence that they were not finished with one another in their hearts.

"Remember to be a member to the thing that once existed."

-Dant Burt

TONYA "KANDIE" THOMAS

CHAPTER 2:

Cheating, Lying & Alcohol

Mom put her domestic duties on the back burner and erupted into a social butterfly. She spent countless hours at her Aunt Bea's (RIP) house after escaping her abusive marriage. That was her place of refuge.

Aunt Bea was Mua's (RIP) older sister. Mr. Husband would not dare go to her house with no mess because he knew what she stood for. Her large frame and feisty demeanor spoke volumes; she was a pistol Pete. Moreover, they were not fans of each other. She and her male friends made bootleg whiskey and it was rumored that Mom was entertaining one of them.

Living in a small town had its share of disadvantages. Everyone knows your business and gossiping was the norm. I believe the women outnumbered the men three to one. With that being said, there was a lot of recycling of men, if you know what I mean. It was no surprise if she or he was with your ex.

Their separation was brewing around town and the

thought of Mom's infidelity infuriated her husband. Although the rumors in the past about Mom and an unknown man were blatant lies.

One evening, Mom got a call that her husband was in the local bar with a woman in a compromising position. As her curiosity began to run wild, Mom went to the bar. In fear of repercussions, she went incognito.

Once in the bar, she noticed her husband with a familiar woman. Witnessing her husband's lustful behavior fueled her pain and seeing how he was captivated by the other woman was heartbreaking.

Mom was having difficulty containing herself, so at the perfect opportunity, she whisked out the bar without blowing her disguise. Not sure how to address the issue, she acted as if it never happened. Ignoring the problem doesn't ease the pain, it intensifies the need to get even.

***

The feeling of hopelessness was too much to bear. Mom started drinking excessively to drown her sorrows and numb the pain. Once the bottle was empty, the problems magnified, and she found herself in the arms of another man.

Hearing the rumors about Mom and her new man was disturbing and Mr. Husband could not contain himself. In his eyes that was the ultimate disrespect. He was good at dishing it out, but accepting his wife in the arms of another man was ludicrous. The little respect that he had for Mom had diminished and he no longer hid the fact that he lived with another woman.

He was what society considered a 'womanizer.'

He showed up to see his kids with his mistress. That spoke volumes about the level of respect he had for his wife and marriage. Not to mention he had the nerve to be feeling some kind of way.

Over time, the hostile environment began to have a profound effect and each of the boys displayed a level of resentment for their dad. This was understandable, since boys tend to gravitate more to their mother.

Princess was the youngest and only girl. Needless to say, as an infant she had her parents wrapped around her finger and she knew it.

Everything she did was "cute" in their eyes.

Although she was cute, her beauty or presence was not enough to hold the marriage together. Their marriage was in a place of despair and their deceitful behavior was destroying the fabric of the family.

***

Mom enjoyed drinking and socializing. She was always the life of the party and very knowledgeable. She could keep the conversation going and had an answer for everything. She would talk you to sleep if you could stand the smell and smoke of those nasty cigarettes. The plot thickened when Mom and the new man were spending more time together because she was no longer hiding her infidelity. They were both officially separated from their spouse with little or no chance of reconciling. They were looking for love in all the wrong places, doing what *felt* good and operating from a place of pain. This meant things were no longer a rumor and she was in fact in an entanglement.

An "Entanglement is a complicated relationship." The 'not knowing' fueled her husband's curiosity and he would stalk her knowingly and unknowingly.

One particular day after a brief surveillance, he noticed one man who caught his eye. He didn't know the man and had never seen him around. During further investigation he found out the man in question was separated from his wife and three daughters, Synil, Joshi and D'Vette; they were from

Cincinnati. He lived with his cousin and worked at the mill.

A few months later, Mr. Husband saw them in the local bar and confronted her with the gossip concerning her new man. Although she denied it, he knew she was lying. Not wanting to show the effects of his bruised ego, he asked her about the kids. She told him they were 'with her mom.'

As she walked away rolling her eyes, he said angrily "You should be home with them!"

Things continued to spiral out of control, and not long afterward, it was rumored that she was pregnant. Not wanting to accept the choices she made, Mom went into denial mode. Ignoring her pregnancy was her way of dealing with it. Mom denied it until she could no longer hide her baby bump.

"Denial is a method of self-protection. You are trying to protect yourself from the truth that is too

painful for you to accept at the moment.
Sometimes short-term denial is essential. It gives you time to organize yourself and accept a significant change in your life."

***

A few weeks later, Mr. Husband saw them being giddy, walking down the street hand in hand. He followed them until he knew exactly where they were going. He hid inside the telephone booth to cut off their path. Once they approached, he jumped out and grabbed Mom as her boyfriend stood watching.

Holding her by her arm, he stared at her protruding stomach. The rage he displayed was unacceptable. He asked her, "Why did you lie about being pregnant?"

Before giving her a chance to respond, he slapped her a few times and said, "Drinking and smoking is not good for the baby!" and then he released her.

As they continued down the street. He yelled and told her, "I will be over tomorrow to see the kids."

Since the separation, he appeared to be more focused on Mom's personal life than the welfare of his kids and wasn't providing as he should have. Once he found out about the new boyfriend, he refused to give Mom money because he realized that he was the only source of income. He neglected the fact that his babies needed food and a roof over their heads.

Denying his babies was not right. Not wanting to see her, he would give Mua the money to give to Mom. The thought of her having another man's child I imagine was devastating since they already had a newborn baby daughter and four boys.

To add insult to the injury he was questioning paternity. Moreover, he was adamant that it was not his child since the dates did not match up and she tried to hide it.

Mom knew as well!

He was presumed to be the father since they were legally married. Pregnancy is supposed to be a joyous time once the shock and morning sickness wears off. During this time, you should focus on having a healthy baby, attending prenatal visits, eating healthy, and not consuming alcohol or smoking. Your body and mind begin to shift in participation for bonding.

The excitement is overwhelming.

Your focus should be the feeling your unborn child growing inside of you, hearing the heartbeat for the first time, and   finding out the gender is mind blowing.

By The time you are in your second trimester, you begin to prepare for your child. Getting the nursery ready, deciding on the theme, and buying all the cute baby clothes. Older siblings are looking forward to the new addition and the family is thinking of names and speculating whose features are going to be dominating.

This is what pregnancy ***should*** be like.

TONYA "KANDIE" THOMAS

CHAPTER 3:

Change

On a very cold winter Thursday morning in January, Mom awakened with intense discomfort. As she tried to go back to sleep, the pain increased. Mom did not want to deal with what was causing the pain, so she laid there in denial attempting to ignore it.

"Avoidance is a defense mechanism people use to avoid feelings or processing difficult and uncomfortable emotions like guilt or shame."

After she could no longer tolerate the pain, she arrived at Northside Hospital. She went through labor, delivery, and recovery by herself. After giving birth to her sixth child, I surmise she felt DEFEATED and alone.

Although she enjoyed all the visitors, she didn't talk much about her new bundle of joy other than it was a girl who she named *Tonya "Kandie" Thomas*.

This is one of the few times Mom was speechless. If you crossed Mom, she would let you know she was confrontational. To show love and support was normal after the birth of a new baby. However, that was not the case.

***

The next several days were chaos with all the gossipers trying to see who or what I looked like. Many of the unwanted visitors went directly to the nursery. They would look at me through the window whispering to one another as they speculated who I looked like. The staring, speculations and unwanted visitors all had toxic energy.

People can be so involved in other people's business that they don't understand the impact it has on everyone involved. This is why I am able to surmise what happened. I felt everything from them except the love of God.

Once all the visitors were gone. Mom laid there in deep thought looking like a deer in the headlights, defeat was written all over her face. She was attempting to come to grips with her new reality. The very thing that she had denied for the past nine months was her innocent beautiful baby girl.

My parents were not ready to deal with the skeleton in their closet. The resentment, abandonment and rejection were evident in their actions. After all, they had been disconnected since my conception.

My father chose not to participate in my birth. He never took Mom or the relationship seriously because it was fun and intriguing at the time. Since they were committing adultery, he was looking for prey and did what most hurt people do....

Hurt people!

Although he only treated her how she allowed. I was their lil secret and he hoped to keep it that way. It was clear to mom that cheating on her husband was her *first* MISTAKE and having unprotected sex with a married man compounded the MISTAKE.

After being discharged from the hospital, my tumultuous journey began. My earliest remembrance is living with my mother and siblings in the notorious Eastside Housing Projects AKA The Kimmel Brooks. It was known for single parent households and at-risk children.

 Living in the inner city had its share of disadvantages: overcrowded living quarters, short food supply, having to fend for yourself at an early age and utilities being disconnected.

The abrupt changes were too much for Mr. Husband, so he was drinking more. He was clueless of how he got there, and this appeared to be his way of coping with the separation.

His presence would infuriate Mom so her attitude would go from 0 to 100 in a second. During those times they didn't agree on anything. As he pulled in the parking lot, Mom would yell up the stairs ``Princess y'all daddy is here."

The three youngest children, Blaze, Princess & I would run down the stairs and Mom would usher us out the door as quickly as she could. LOL. She didn't want to look at him as we all eagerly hurried out to the parking lot to greet him.

Princess would run past me in full pursuit, chuckling and saying, "My daddy is here, my daddy is here!!" She would then look over to gauge my reaction; she was so messy. She would turn to Blaze and say, "Daddy is here."

Needless to say, it took every ounce of strength to hold my composer, although I never gave her the reaction she was looking for. Her callous, vindictive remark pierced my heart and has forever resonated in my spirit. The malice she harbored towards me was mind blowing.

As I looked over at their dad the look on his face was priceless and the impact was devasting. It was not a pretty picture; nothing was cute about it or her. As a parent and an adult, he was supposed to chastise her.

I turned away, fighting back tears with my head held down and rolling my eyes. I realize she thrived on torturing me and Mom and her "Dad" were in cahoots since they condoned her distasteful comments.

She did no wrong in their eyes.

Whenever I would tell them, they would say, "Quit being a tattle tale." That was their way of deflecting.

'Dad' would embrace me with a big hug as he attempted to persuade me. Maybe he thought that softened the blow. I am grateful for his love and wished he would have not allowed her to sabotage our relationship.

It was more painful knowing my feelings were not being validated. It has always been a pet peeve to know my thoughts and views were invalid and to insist on me seeing things differently and to their advantage.

"Energy is ELECTRIFYING." It cannot be hidden or overlooked.

~Tonya "Kandie" Thomas

REFLECTION:

Take a moment to think about a scandal that you were a part of. How did you respond? Was it valid? If not, hold yourself accountable to do the right thing.

You may need to pray or ask for forgiveness. Whatever it is, free yourself; only you can change.

I was prejudged long before I was formed in my mother's womb. I had no way of expressing myself and I was not given a fair chance.

***

Princess had a difficult time processing that she was no longer the baby of the family or the only girl. It was apparent that she was jealous.

"Jealousy is a complex emotion that typically arises when a person perceives a threat to a valued relationship from a third party."

I went to my bedroom feeling dejected with no place to turn. Once in my bedroom, **I looked out the window**. I could see Princess sitting on her dad's lap acting like she was driving (that's cute). He was in total awe.

Blaze was standing by the car looking annoyed throwing rocks. As I went to the bathroom, I could see Mom standing in the door smoking a cigarette and watching. She looked up at me as I was whimpering and wiping my tears, yet she never said a word.

Shortly afterwards, she came to my bedroom as I was looking out the window. She walked over and peeked out. I turned to tell her what happened, expressing to her how I felt about their choice of words.

"Princess, y'all dad," meaning her and Blaze.

Princess responded back with excitement, "*My* dad!" Implying only her dad.

Big MISTAKE on my part to think Mom cared about me or *my* feelings. She never showed me any love or affection. She went up one side of me and came down the other. It was like pouring accelerant on a raging fire.

I couldn't believe her reaction.

I stood there in disbelief crying and sobbing. Not to mention my tears did not phase her, they became her ammunition. The harder and louder my cries, the more she went in.

As she turned to leave the room she blurred out, "You are always looking for a reason to cry and if you don't shut up, I will give you something to cry about!"

As I am trying to muffle my cries. I realized; Princess was mimicking Mom's behavior. All I could think about was why am I being treated in such a despicable manner? What have I done? Why is Blaze annoyed? Why does Princess act if she is entitled? Why is she getting all the attention? Why are they allowing it? Why is everything Princess does so cute? Why? Tell me Why!

Although those were my thoughts, I never shared my feelings due to fear of the unknown. What I do know is my presence made a negative impact on their ideal family and I didn't deserve to be treated like a stray animal. Being the youngest I took the brunt of the punishment. We are all close in age and have our own unique personality.

As I was taking notice of what was happening around me, it was not hard to identify what was going on. Mom was the lead player to this chaotic madness they called 'family.' Princess was easily influenced, and she influenced our brothers; they are not as cruel but the disconnect was obvious.

They view me as a MISTAKE.

***

Mom had an adulterous affair that led to her divorce, which triggered Princess's condescending behavior and played a vital role in our siblingship. I am talking about how someone can have so much power.

LOL! After all, she is their "PRINCESS." (ROLLING MY EYES)

Basil was a gem; his nurturing abilities were amazing considering he was a kid himself. He was the epitome of what a big brother should be: loving, compassionate, and giving. I am forever grateful for his love.

The second child Donald (RIP) was territorial and withdrawn. He appeared to be unapproachable and angry.

He had little to no respect for Mom, Dad, and the authorities. He was the only child in our house who was allowed to have his own bedroom. He took the knob off the door and booby trapped it.

No one would dare mess with him or his belongings. One day I asked Mom, "Why does he have his own bedroom?"

She responded in a loud derogatory manner, "Why

are you in other people's business?"

Biker is the third child. He is a comedian at heart with flat jokes. That is his way of deflecting. Him and I were never close since he and Princess have always acted as though they are Siamese twins, identical twin, fraternal twins, and Irish twins all in one. We know this is medically impossible since he is three years her senior.

I used this analogy to equate how strong their love and bond has always been. Not to mention they even look like they could be fraternal twins.

Blaze the fourth boy is two years my senior. He is radical and known for being loud and aggressive. He was always rough playing with me. He would hold me down and cover my mouth. I did not like being restrained, so I would fight with all my strength to get loose. All the while he would laugh and get a kick out of it. This was the only issue he and I had.

Moreover, looking back at it, he was the only one in the house who interacted with me. He appeared to have a chip on his shoulder towards Dad. I surmise he resented how Dad was treating Mom. The level of disrespect he and Donald had for 'Dad' was evident in their actions. Dad often spoke about it and Mom could care less.

Princess is the oldest girl and fifth child. She is my Irish twin and their love child. You are probably thinking, Irish twin? Right, it has nothing to do with ethnicity or sharing the womb.

"Irish twins are siblings who are born within twelve months of one another."

"She is deceitful!" Yes, and I repeat, "She is a deceitful two-faced habitual liar."

She thrived on chaos and has been proven to be the best at it. With us being so close in age, it saddens me to say my BIG sister despises me. What is more disturbing is that she is known to be everything I called her.

I have always opened my heart to extend my love. I pray that she has a 'come to Jesus moment' so her hardened heart can be softened. Before you begin to pass judgment, remember this is *my* story and **MY TRUTH**.

"God granted me the serenity to accept the things I cannot change, the courage to change the things I can and the wisdom to know the difference."

***

As I walked by Mua's house, I noticed her and her neighbor watering their grass. After waving at them,

I ran and gave her a big hug. They told me that I looked pretty in my new overall outfit and sandals. As I was thanking them for the compliment. Uncle Black's girlfriend came to the door.

She said, "Kandie, you look pretty."

I thanked her and she asked me if she could comb my hair. I happily said, "Yes." When she was done, I thanked her for doing my hair.

Mua had made dinner and I loved her signature neckbones with rice and tomatoes. After eating, it was time to go home. On my way home I saw Princess and her posse. Everyone except for her told me my hair was pretty. It was obvious I had just got it combed. Since it was out of the norm, I thanked them.

Princess asked, "Who did your hair?" with an attitude. I told her and when I got home, she was already there. I walked in the door; I could tell they were up to no good. Mom asked me who combed my hair. I told her uncle Black's girlfriend. As she was cussing me out, she hit me with an orange racetrack. The orange racetrack was from the boys' hot wheel track and Mom used it to whip us. Before I knew it, she had whacked me. I flinched and she jumped.

That was my reflex.

She said, "Girl you will draw back a nub."

Princess ran her scary instigating butt up the stairs. She knew she was wrong, and I was wrong as well. I often wished I had alerted the authorities.

***

Mua would check on us to make sure we had the necessary essentials. Mom was her third child, yet she adored all her children having twelve of her own.

Mua felt compelled to assist. She didn't like us borrowing from neighbors, that was one of her many pet peeves.

Her house was a place of refuge where I could escape the torture and she knew my pain. She was aware of Mom's indiscretions, so she would comfort and console me.

I avoided going over to Mua's house when Auntie Diva was home. She is Mom's baby sister, and she was looking forward to graduating from high school and moving to California. She ran the house like a boot camp with her dominating personality.

She would fly off the hook and say things to make me feel like I was responsible for my mom's irresponsible parenting. Mua allowed her to take charge, which is how she got her name (Diva/ Mama).

"A 'Diva' is a woman who is perceived as self-absorbed. She has self-confidence, self-respect and hella swagger. She knows who she is and exactly

---

where she is going. Her style and attitude are on point even when she is noy trying."

I always admired her beauty, poise, and integrity. Her elegance speaks for itself. She has a way of commanding the room when she enters.

I tried to minimize my visits knowing it would cause problems which made me feel terrible. However, sometimes dealing with the chaos left me no choice. The thought of her moving in a few months was saddening.

The excitement she displayed in anticipation of the move was amazing. Everything I had heard about California was on television, books, or magazines. It all appeared glamorous. From the movie stars to the modern style homes, flashy cars, and red carpets. I was happy and sad for the obvious because California was far away.

I would ask her questions like, "Are you going to see movie stars? Are you going to the beach? Will I see you on The Price is Right Show?"

She smirked she said, "Nah girl."

I was thinking, "You got what it takes!"

***

One day I was outside playing and one of my neighbors told me about the card party Mom had planned for later that evening. In the 70s, this was the way to make extra money.

Mom's hustle was epic, and she was known for hosting a card party. It would be 'lit' for lack of a better term. Playing Bid Whist, shooting dice, selling dinners and alcoholic beverages was Mom's favorite pastime. The Kimmel Brooks were a family within itself where everyone looked out for each other and knew each other's indiscretions.

She was older, so I guess that explains why she knew what was happening at my house. As the day progressed, I noticed Mom was preparing for the party. She was cooking, cleaning, and making sure she had spare change. Once the party started, us kids were upstairs confined to our bedrooms. We would hear loud music playing and different voices. Some of them were unrecognized so we would attempt to guess who it was. That was our way of seeing who was downstairs as well as overhearing adult conversations.

Whenever we wanted to be nosey, we would go to the bathroom or if we were bold enough, we would go downstairs to the refrigerator for some water. Needless to say, I didn't have to sneak, Mom was always calling me to come downstairs. She would ask me, "Do you remember Mr. or Miss so and so?" They overlooked me and not in a good way, although I was clueless for a brief minute.

After being called down about the third time, it became evident. As I was going up the stairs. I could hear adult conversations regarding my paternity. This made the hairs on the back of my neck stand up.

I went to my bedroom feeling like a MISFIT as I stored the unsavory information in the archives of my mind with all the other awful comments from Princess.

Once the party was over, we kids would hurry downstairs to find money laying around as well as people sleeping in chairs at the table and on the sofa. We would pocket the money then hurry back to our bedroom. Although no one ever said to me directly that Mr. Husband was not my dad, Princess made it clear every chance she got. Mr. Husband tried to hide his feelings, but the agony was more than he was willing to accept.

Which was understanding.

He was coming over less and less trying to minimize the pain. Over time, he felt compelled to be my dad, seeing how nonchalant and neglectful my biological father was.

A few weeks later, Dad made prior arrangements with Mom, and she was aware that his girlfriend would be picking us up and taking us school shopping. Once she arrived, Mom hollered up the stairs. "Princess y'all daddy's girlfriend is out there!"

As we hurried out the door, Mom would usher us out the door yelling obscenities. I walked to the car feeling apprehensive with my head hung down. As I got closer, I looked up at Ms. Girlfriend who was sitting patiently waiting for us, with a big warm and lovable smile.

She was happy to see us, and the feelings were mutual. As I got closer to the car, I could hear Mom saying unpleasant things in hopes of getting a reaction. Ms. Girlfriend never so much as even looked at her. She was an educator, and she would talk to us about school and its importance.

Hours later during the ride home, I felt happy, loved, and grateful for my new clothes and shoes. As we nervously approached our neighborhood, I recall thinking this was really nice of her. Once we pulled into the parking space, it was little or no talk. We always hurried in and out.

***

The summer prior to kindergarten, I got more exposure. What I mean by that is I was starting to play outside with my friends unattended. It was approved by my mom if I followed her rules. No matter what I was doing, I was obedient. The rules where you better hear me when I call you or else and you better be in the house when the streetlights come on.

Needless to say, I did not venture far in fear of repercussions. The whack from the orange racetrack was a constant reminder. Realizing Mom was eyeing the big orange racetracks, I didn't say another word. The orange racetrack was separated from the boys' hot wheel track. That is what Mom used to whip us with.

I prided myself on being on my best behavior.

The verbal and mental abuse was more than I could handle. Mom's loud, vulgar voice was intimidating, not to mention she hated me. All the lies, stress and lack of love had my anxiety at a peak.

"Anxiety is a feeling of nervousness or unease typically about an imminent event or something with an uncertain outcome."

It was clear that I was a non-factor. Feeling ostracized made me feel trapped in a corner with no place to turn.

Tawanna Madison and her family lived close to us and Mom was friends with her grandmother and mother.

She had a large extended family and we always had fun playing all kinds of games like 'red light green light,' 'mother may I,' 'say say say,' 'Mary Mack' and many others.

Those were the fun times.

They were from down south Tallulah, Louisiana, and their energy was electrifying. I loved their sweet spirit and country dialect. Other times. I would be on the back porch playing 'Jax' with my next-door neighbor.

She was a recluse who didn't socialize with many people. Her youngest brother and I would go get the daily newspaper for the elderly lady and elderly man down the way. They would award us with a baggie full of assorted candy and we looked forward to the reward.

The Sunday newspaper costs more and is much larger and heavier with all the sale ads, so we received extra on those days. Early one Sunday morning as I was walking down the street, I saw a well-dressed older man in a new Cadillac. He was talking to the kids while they were waiting on the church bus. Several men were on the corner shooting dice, and mothers would be coming home after being out all night with their shoes in their hands. Some kids were outside with the same clothes as the day before.

Later that day, everyone was playing and talking about the first day of school approaching. All the kids were excited as they shared their views on each teacher. With everyone trying to talk at once it was difficult to understand what was being said. As I tentatively listened to the conversation and watched as they thoroughly explained, it was like watching a good tennis match.

My friends and I could not respond since this would be our first year. When my friends and I would ask a question, the older kids would ignore us or lick out their tongues to taunt us, calling us, "Kindergarten babies, stick your head in gravy."

After tentatively listening, the directions were simple and clear: go to the far end of the building to the large double doors. Line up close to the wall and wait quietly for your teacher. I stood there thinking, "No big deal."

They stated that Ms. Kinder was an awesome teacher and a fixture in the community. She also lived in the neighborhood in the large red brick house on Republic Avenue with the golf course and all the fruit trees.

The night before, Mom hot combed Princess and my hair. She complained the whole time she was doing mine and I got burnt several times, claiming I was moving and saying, "Your hair makes my fingers cramp."

This was all while chain smoking those nasty stinky cigarettes and blowing the smoke in my face. Once she was done and my hair was tied up, I laid in bed with my pillow over my face to muffle my cries. She was always mean to me! Burning ME!

While she was doing Princess's long thick coarse hair, I could hear them laughing and giggling. When Princess was not crying, or if Mom was trying to pacify her; that's cute since she was tender headed.

That seems like the longest night ever.

After a long sleepless night, I anticipated going to kindergarten at Harrison Elementary School.

"Kindergarten is a time when five-year-olds interact with each other for developmental growth. Playtime is transformed  *into opportunities to instill cognitive skills, motor skills and social skills."*

72

My anxiety was at an all-time high and I was a ball of emotions. I lay there pondering what had been spoken and I was looking forward to a change.

As I brushed my teeth in preparation for my first day of kindergarten, I could see the burns on my scalp, ear, and forehead from the hot comb. I was pissed and upset! Mom was  making breakfast, which was not normal in our house, then she rushed us out the door.

As my older brothers, sister and I started out the door, she made it clear she was glad summer was over so she could have some free time. We saw our neighbors Sally, Billy and everyone was dressed nicely; we were all excited and well behaved.

We had to walk past two crossing guards to get to school. We did not take the shortcut through the woods because no one wanted to get dirt and weeds

73

on their new shoes and clothes. It felt good to be out of that house and out of Mom's presence.

I didn't say much, I enjoyed the tranquility! I had been looking forward to this day forever: the much-needed change.

Once we made it to the campus. I went to the far end of the building where my fellow classmates were standing in line. As I was walking to the end of the line, I noticed several familiar faces. Mee Mee, Kim, Toni, Anne, and Wesley were talking and laughing.

Several parents waited with their child. When the bell rang, Ms. Kinder came out and led us into the classroom. She was tentative and compassionate with an uplifting spirit. Once in the classroom I became withdrawn and territorial.

The huge classroom was breathtaking and was divided into two parts. The playroom was sectioned off with a kitchen set filled with dishes and play food.

There were also tricycles, baby dolls, cars, and trucks for our enjoyment.

This was all new to me. There were too many students and too much movement. I was out of my **ELEMENT,** and I felt outnumbered and overwhelmed.

After school, I would walk home with my classmates. Most of their parents would be standing outside waiting for them when the bell rang. Others would be waiting in their car. Mom would walk and meet me sometimes if she was not watching her soap operas: 'All My children,' 'One Life To Live' and 'General Hospital.' She was more concerned about what was going on in Luke's and Laura's life that she didn't have time for Kandie.

"A mother's duties are limitless; she will sacrifice her love and life. A mother's love is one of the first indications of the sovereignty of God."

The first week of school was behind me and it wasn't so bad after all. More so, it was fun learning, sharing, and playing and I met several new friends. With school being my outlet, I was vigilant and looked forward to going.

***

One day in class as we were lining up, Mee Mee beat me to the line. Needless to say, I was mad, so I punched her in her stomach. I didn't think I had hit her that hard, however the grunt and her reactions spoke volumes to the impact of my blow.

As she cried, I apologized, and she accepted. After all, my adjustment proved to be a challenge. I was wrong and she didn't deserve it.

Ms Kinder called me to her desk to reprimand me and I noticed she was holding a ruler. She held my hand and asked, "Would you like a milkshake?"

Of course, I said, "Yes."

She replied, "**Good,** what kind do you like?'

While I am thinking, she says, "I am going to give you a strawberry milkshake, burger and fries."

I was thinking how nice of her until she whacked me twice on my hand and I had to sit in the hot seat. This was my punishment for punching my classmate. I was set apart from the rest of the class for the remainder of the day and I was livid. I felt like a spectacle in that large open classroom of thirty kids.

Needless to say, Mee Mee and I became friends. She was skinny, nice, and pretty with two long ponytails. She spoke with a soft voice and an angelic smile. We would play together at home because our brothers were good friends.

Wow! What a year.

***

Now that I had successfully pressed my way through kindergarten... Yes! I said pressed!

School was my place of peace and I enjoyed learning, playing, and sharing. Change was needed and it made all the difference. The abuse was a hindrance and caused me to be timid and guarded; I could not function at my fullest potential. During summer break, I began to run amuck around the Brooks. There was never a dull moment.

One of my classmate's mothers was shot through the mailbox and killed. A friend was accidentally shot inside her home and became paralyzed, and my youngest sister and her friend found a dead body in the woods.

Seeing the red and blue flashing lights from the police car and hearing the ambulance siren was exciting to me. Eric Lott, Mee Mee, Kipper, and Mack would run in full strife in pursuit of knowing what was happening. Not to mention it was exciting to know what was going on.

There would be every bae bae and their momma in attendance. The local newspaper and news channel would film and interview while us unruly kids would be jumping in front of the camera hoping to see ourselves when the story aired.

Once the excitement was over, we hung out on the barrels playing tag. When I went home, Mom was getting ready to leave.

She asked me, "Did you hear me calling you?

I said, "No."

As I was explaining that I was up the street with Princess and Blaze she said, "I didn't ask you about them."

She lit a cigarette and told me to come with her. Unsure of what was going on, after a long ride we pulled into the driveway at Aunt Bea's house. Aunt Bea, her dog and a male friend were there

TONYA "KANDIE" THOMAS

CHAPTER 4:

The Need To

Be Loved

Mom had oral surgery. While she was recovering, she needed some TLC, so we went to Mua's house.

Mua and Auntie Diva were tentative to her needs although she slept most of the day. Other than the frequent moans and the spitting up of blood, she was on the road to recovery. Seeing Mom in intense pain broke my heart. I wished that there was something I could do to relieve her pain.

As I played quietly with the 'mysterious little girl,' who I thought may be my younger cousin, was two years my junior. She didn't talk much, and she was pretty and chocolate. She looked like a black cabbage doll.

I knew she wasn't auntie's daughter since auntie didn't have any kids. Although I watched her bathe, potty train and comb her hair with all those pretty colorful hair ribbons and barrettes, she adored her like a mother should. I always wondered what the connection was. No one explained, and like always,

I never asked in fear of being cussed out and yelled at. Not to mention she lived with them.

I felt bewildered, deeply, and utterly confused. Henceforth I enjoyed our bonding time. We played with her baby dolls, kitchen set and fake food.

Later that day, there was a knock on the door. Mua looked through the peephole and motioned for Mom to go to the bedroom, so Mom and I went into the bedroom.

Shortly afterwards, we could hear laughing and talking. Mom motioned for me to be quiet as she tried to hear what was being said, standing closer to the door. She could not hear clearly, so she took the empty drinking glass off the dresser and placed it against the wall, pressing her ear against it. After trying several times, she still could not hear clearly.

I looked over at her facial expression and it was obvious she was experiencing some adverse reactions from the surgery and needed her barf can. I quickly went to retrieve it from the living room. As I opened the bedroom door I glanced and could see an older man who looked like a church deacon. He was dressed in a nice suit with a hat and holding the 'mysterious child."

Not wanting to be a distraction, I grabbed the can and hurried to give it to Mom. Before I could hand Mom her barf can, she snatched it out of my hands without saying thank you.

She was always heartless towards me.

He didn't stay long and once he left, we went back into the living room. The 'mysterious child' was happier than usual, and she had several dollar bills in her hands.

I sat quietly trying to figure out what his connection was. Other than 'mysterious child' being giddy it was like sitting in a room with three mannequins. No one said a thing and Moms' energy was toxic. The unpleasant expression on Mom's face made her look suspect.

Shortly after, I began to ponder... Who is this man? And who did he come to visit? Thinking he appeared to be too old for Auntie Diva and he referred to Mua as Ms. Ruby.

As Mom sat there rolling her eyes at 'mysterious child' and myself, I was not sure why she was looking at us like that. However, if looks could **KILL,** we both would have been **DEAD**!

The fact that he was holding her was even more confusing. I could not get that picture out of my mind. Suddenly my mind shifted, and I recalled seeing him a few weeks earlier as I was walking from getting the newspaper.

Fast forward…

Several days later, my friends and I were crossing the street to go to the recreation center. Mr. Deacon was driving by, and he waved at us. As we crossed the street in front of him, I could see my reflection on his car. Seeing him in a shiny new Cadillac

I thought, "Wow!" He must be rich.

My friends knew him, and they spoke about him and his shortcomings. I could not believe what I was hearing. I never commented and I would not dare tell them about our brief encounter. In fact, what I thought about him was the total opposite: he was not a church deacon. He was an older married man and the owner of the local bars.

Now I couldn't get that Mr. Deacon or the man who adored me out of my mind. I knew it was a connection. I couldn't get that picture out of my mind. I couldn't forget the brief encounters. From the way 'mysterious' behaved to the way he looked at her.

Once I got home, I went straight to my bedroom. Mom yelled for me to come downstairs. As I hurried downstairs, I was thinking, "What have I done?"

When I arrived downstairs, I noticed she was standing there with something in her hand. As I walked towards her, I could see she was holding a hairbrush. She told me, "Come get your hair brushed."

When she was done, she instructed me to wash my face and put some lotion on my 'ashy' face and legs. As she exited the front door, she never said a word.

When I was done, I followed her out to the parking lot where Uncle Midnight was waiting in his car. Once Mom and I got in, I remember thinking about the last time I was in tow: where we went and who was there.

During the long ride, no one uttered a word. Soon the surroundings became clear. When we arrived, the dog was barking. As I walked into the house, I could tell something was amiss because everyone looked baffled. The man in the uniform shirt spoke with a big inviting smile, just like before. He appeared to adore me.

Before I knew it, he had me on his leg giving me a helicopter ride. I must admit I enjoyed it and all the attention, however there was something amiss. The chemistry with him and Mom was noticeable.

Their shifty eyes and body language were electrifying, yet no one said a word. When he put me down, he gave me two dollars and some candy. I nervously walked over to the sofa and sat next to Mom.

After a few seconds, Uncle Midnight asked Mom was she ready to go. She said, "Yes." So, we got in the car and left. During the car ride home, other than the radio it was quiet. I sat there trying to figure out the connection. I could not get the thought out of my head of how he looked at me and held me. Before long, I drifted off to sleep.

MISTAKES ARE MADE FOR *a reason*

***

When we arrived home, I exited the car and there was a group of kids playing a game of 'kick the can.' While I was walking, I took a second look and noticed that Princess was not there. I was thinking "Good!"

This was my thought because I didn't want to see her. I didn't like her ways because she was always mean. She would bully me and call me names when she was around her friends.

When the game was over, everyone walked to the Jones' family because they had a candy house where they sold lots of goodies. One of my favorites was the caramel candy apples.

As I reached in my pocket, I pulled out the money that the strange man gave me. I bought a soda and a candy apple. It was starting to get late; the streetlights would be coming on soon and everyone was going home.

Once inside the house, I hurried straight to my bedroom thinking about what happened at Aunt Bea's house. I began thinking who was that man? Why was he holding me? Why didn't Mom say anything? More so, it was taboo in our family for little girls to be too friendly with men and sitting on a man's lap was not heard of.

It was hard for me to process my feelings. The mental venom was polluting my spirit and poisoning my soul. Establishing my boundaries taught me to choose my battles. My bedroom was my place of serenity.

"Serenity is the state of being calm, peaceful and untroubled."

***

I thought if I stayed in my bedroom I would be out of harm's way. There were times that I only left the bedroom to go to the bathroom, and no one missed me. However, sharing my bedroom with Princess gave her the liberty to come and go as she pleased. She would antagonize me at every opportunity with her impromptu entrance.

Mom would yell at us to keep our junkie room clean. I always tried to explain to her that those were Princess' dirty clothes and hair accessories on the floor. She would block me out or talk over me as always; she was rude. She knew that I was neat and organized and her little Princess was just like her: messy and disorganized.

Princess would go as far as deliberately wetting my bed as if I peed the bed. Then she would run and tell Mom, "Kandie peed in the bed."

Mom never asked any questions or went to check. She would start cussing and yelling out of control. Princess would be standing there with a big deceitful grin showing her big buck teeth and Mom knew she was lying. I would think to myself, "This is as barbaric as it can get," crying with tears rolling down my face.

I began to feel like a prisoner in my own home. I would be in the bedroom looking out the window or reading my only two Judy Blume books.

One day, I awakened to an eerie quiet house. I turned to see Princess was not in her bed. I rushed over to the window to look out. No one was outside so I hurried down the stairs.

As I peeked in Mom's room, she was asleep. I was careful not to make too much noise and turned on the television to watch my favorite show: The Electric Company.

"The Electric Company used 'comedy' to boost kids' reading skills. Its target audience was elementary students that were too old for Sesame Street but still needed help with learning and reading."

This was one of the few times that I was able to watch it. Since no one else liked it and we only had one television.

A few minutes later the show was over, and no one had come home. I checked on Mom and She was still sleeping, snoring like a bear.

I ran into the kitchen and made myself a bowl of cereal. I sat down and peacefully enjoyed an episode of 'Schoolhouse Rock.' The show was 'appropriate' for ages three to thirteen. I enjoyed learning about conjunctions and their functions.

"Conjunctions are parts of speech that connect words, phrases, clauses, or sentences."

The most common conjunction that was used in our house were 'was' and 'but.' I heard 'but' for Kandie this or that so much I wanted to change my name.

I was always ostracized so the program was very informative and gave me clarity. It talked about likes and differences.

I put Basil, Donald, and myself together and asked the question, "What was like vs difference?"

Then I did it with Biker, Blaze, and myself. Same question, different people, same results. I sat there in total awe trying to wrap my mind around the facts that illuminated my mind.

Needless to say, the like vs difference was obvious when it came to Princess and me. That episode made me realize I have two functions: propel or derail. It solidified my thoughts and feelings.

Later that day, Mr. Husband's sister Aunt Bunny and sister-in-law Aunt Passion came over to tell Mom his dad had passed away. She wanted to make sure **WE** looked nice for 'our grandfather's' home going service.

She asked if she could take Princess and myself shopping to get an outfit and Mom said yes. When it was time to pay, Aunt Bunny refused to pay for my stuff, so Aunt Passion pulled out her credit card and paid for my belongings. She hugged me and I thanked her.

Shortly afterwards, we headed to the car. Princess had several bags and insisted on carrying them by herself. She was always catty. With Princess' spiteful behavior, I was able to put things in perspective.

I was bothered by all her shenanigans and tired of all the gaslighting. I wanted to be loved and embraced the same way Princess was.

Once we arrived home, Princess hurried into the house to show off her new wardrobe. I went straight upstairs to my bedroom.

While Princess had her own little fashion show, I was sitting in my bedroom listening tentatively to what was going on downstairs. I waited on Mom to ask me what I got, but needless to say she never did. Other than laughing, all I heard was 'that's cute.' That was the norm when it came to Princess; everything was *cute*.

It had gotten quiet downstairs and I began to drift off to sleep. Not long afterwards, Princess turned on the light as she entered the room to put her stuff away. I didn't want to see or hear her, so I went to the bathroom.

A few seconds later, Princess started knocking on the door. I told her I would be out in a minute. She began to tug at the door saying it was urgent. I repeated myself, "I will be out in a minute."

At that point, she was screaming, "I have to go!"

I hurried to exit the bathroom feeling annoyed and went downstairs. As I began telling Mom what happened while we were shopping with Aunt Bunny, I told her what she said, "My brother is not Kandie's daddy, and I am not buying her stuff!"

Princess came running downstairs in full pursuit.

She never went into the bathroom or said a word. She stood there with her big teeth and that stupid grin on her face.

Mom began yelling at me saying, "I can't tell anybody what to do with their money," while she eyed the orange racetrack. She never acknowledged what was said.

She was always deflecting.

"Deflecting typically appears when a person is confronted with their mistakes. Instead of accepting responsibility and facing uncomfortable situations head-on. The deflector will try to move the focus from themselves, usually by passing the blame onto someone or something else."

TONYA "KANDIE" THOMAS

It wasn't even about the money.

She completely disregarded the statement and my feelings. As I went to my bedroom to gather my thoughts, I had a plethora of emotions, and my mind was running rampant. I began thinking things like…..

"This is what all the talk was about. This is why you are not with your husband. This is why you called me down the stairs. This is why I felt like a spectacle, and you treated me differently. This is why I was ostracized by my siblings."

I was old enough for Mom to have a conversation with me, but she never has. She has always had a hidden agenda. This is why Princess always made it clear she was her daddy's baby and 'only' girl.

As my mind went from one emotion to another, I began thinking, "This is why you viewed me as a *mistake*."

My thoughts became clear.

Mom and Mr. Husband's sister Aunt Bunny had a baby with her brother and vice versa. They were ***always*** in their brother's business.

"If it doesn't come out in the wash, it will come out in the dry."

– Judge Lauren Lake

***

Being victimized at the hands of my parents for many years was appalling. It was hurtful knowing they despised me.

I was bewildered.

Being in a state of confusion, I never shared my thoughts with Mom. Consequently, everything I had believed was true. It was very hurtful not being able to talk with Mom about the whole situation because of how she addressed the issues; this spoke volumes to me. I went straight to my bedroom trying to process the information.

I will never know.

Message To My Father:

How come you denied me?
How come you never acknowledged your baby girl?
How come you held me and smiled in my face?
How come you never spoke a word?
How come you left me with all these
unanswered questions?
Daddy how come?
How come? How come?

Unfortunately, there was no love, protection, or provision when it came to Kandie. Henceforth Mom never spoke about it. I would not dare bring up that topic with her again.

MISTAKES ARE MADE FOR *a reason*

***

Mom continued to neglect her kids and responsibilities and regularly hosted card parties. This kept her mom home, yet Auntie Diva moved to California, and everyone appeared to be sad. She was always stern and sweet.

The love I have for her cannot be explained and she has never missed my birthday. Thanks again for the angel coin pennant you gave me in 2001, I still carry it in my wallet.

The next few years were traumatic without Auntie Diva. She was one of the few people who allowed me to vent without passing judgment and always had an encouraging word.

After hundreds of questions, she would say to me, "DANG KANDIE quit asking so many questions!!' LOL!!

TONYA "KANDIE" THOMAS

That's LOVE!

My siblings were never tentative to me and my needs when Mom would be in her bedroom sleeping or passed out on the couch.

Basil and his friends would be in and out of the house and Donald (RIP) would have a room full of boys playing the electric football game. Biker would be outside with his best friend tinkering with his bike. He has always taken pride in his bike.

Princess would be on the back porch keeping him company, being fast and enticing his friend. Princess and Biker have always been close.

Blaze would be somewhere cussing someone out. He was known for being in mischief. Being the youngest at the time I took the brunt of the punishment. I was mentally bullied.

***

Years later, I recall Mua saying she would be moving

to California due to health reasons. The thought of her leaving made me sad and uneasy. As time went by, she was packing, shipping, and giving stuff away. Before I knew it, the house was bare from wall to wall. Soon I realized I would have to fin for myself. Aunt Diva had already left and now Mua leaving hit me like a ton of bricks.

Moving day came.

We all went to the Trailway Bus station and packed into that small, confined space like sardines. Everyone was crying and hugging Mua, Aunt Bea, 'mysterious child,' and my two younger cousins who were heading to Sacramento California. Since Aunt Bea was in a wheelchair and had difficulty walking it prolonged our goodbyes; we all embraced the moment.

Shortly afterwards, the bus finished boarding. The cries got louder, and the hugs got tighter. Finally, the bus was ready to leave, and the door closed. As we were waving and crying, the bus took off. When we looked up, Precious was screaming and crying out of control chasing the bus.

We all laughed.

That was a site to see: her little chubby self-chasing the bus. Now ***that*** was cute! I point that out to show how much of an impact Mua had in her short life.

When we finally got home, the house was quiet and still. That's a first. With everyone home, no one said a word. For the next few weeks we tried to adjust to Mua being gone. Without saying we missed her we would talk about how Precious looked so cute chasing after the bus. That was a priceless moment.

My Grandfather aka 'Da,' Uncle Alvin, Uncle Suave and Uncle Midnight would come over several times a week. Most of the time mom was gone.

They would always ask, "Where is your mom?"

I always had the same response. I would shrug my

shoulders as if to say, "I don't know."

They would shake their head with a look of dismay on their face as they replied she should be home soon.

Da' always had a can of 7up and He would say

"Candy bar, get a cup so I can give you some of this pop."

He always called me Candy bar and it made me feel special.

Uncle Suave would give us a lecture about staying in the house and not opening the door.

One particular time, he came and brought groceries. Once he placed the grocery bags on the countertop, I hurried to see what he brought. As I took the food out of the bags, I noticed he brought my favorite and least favorite.

He saw my reactions when I picked up the Salisbury steak entrees; Salisbury steak boiling bags were my favorite. I continued unpacking the bag and noticed the top ramen noodles I didn't care for. He always said the same thing: put the food away, don't mess with the stove and your mom will be home soon.

I thought, "How do you know? You didn't even know she was gone."

He was a bit flashy, well dressed in nice loud colored suits and wore hats to match. He drove a blue Cadillac with an antenna on the back window and he looked like he had money. I would ask him for a dollar. He would complain but he gave it to me. That was nice of him.

I have always loved and appreciated him.

Uncle Clean (RIP) is the oldest. He was always dressed to kill. He came over a few times with his wife. She was beautiful and dressed well.

When I told him Mom was not home, he said he knew where to find her. As I watched him leave, I thought, "He is richer than Uncle Suave and Mr. Deacon."

They looked like NEW MONEY!

***

During an overnight visit to my Aunt Ellen's (RIP) house, I thought it was a bad nightmare. I was awakened during a nap screaming as Princess buried my face under a big bulky sofa pillow and she laid her body over me.

I was kicking and screaming in total fear.

This was happening while my teenage cousin's long ridged fingernails scratched and penetrated the surface of my vagina like tiger's claws.

As I cried and kicked, I could hear them talking and laughing. When I thought the ordeal was over, they attempted to make his friend join in. During the debate, they diverted their attention to his friend. That's when I made a quick dash up the stairs.

As I was fleeing, I looked over at the dining room table and saw Uncle Ned there in a drunken stupor pissing on the floor. I hurried to the bathroom with Princess in close pursuit.

I locked the door.

Princess kept knocking on the door asking if I wanted to play hide and seek, as if nothing ever happened. I told her, "No," as she persisted asking and knocking.

Before long, she unlocked the door and was inside the bathroom standing there with her big teeth and smudge demeanor. I wanted to bash her head in. She had the audacity to ask, "Why don't you want to play? Why are you crying?"

Feeling like I needed a bath and medical attention, the intense whimpering and hyperventilating was bothersome. Moreover, a bath was not an option. I would not dare disrobe around those molesters.

MISTAKES ARE MADE FOR *a reason*

***

The next day when I went home, I was scared to tell Mom. I could hardly walk, and she didn't notice.

I went to my bedroom feeling defeated and dealing with the same scenario: Princess and her antagonist behavior. She went back and forth trying to gauge my behavior. She sat there watching me and never said a word.

I left and went to the bathroom, which was the only place I had privacy. Before long she was knocking and turning the doorknob saying, "Kandie I got to use the bathroom."

I told her, "I will be out in a minute," as she continued her shenanigans.

Mom stood at the bottom of the stairs yelling for me to come out. I hurried out hoping she would notice something was wrong. When she didn't, that intensified my anger.

That was when I blurted out what happened. "Princess held me down while your nephew put his fingers in my private."

She did not seem surprised. She cussed me out, and said, "You probably were over there being fast. That's what you get. Now get out of my f*!@*! face, and don't breathe those f*!@*! words no more in life."

I stood there in total disbelief.

When she finished cussing, I wanted to run but I couldn't, but instead I hurried to my bedroom. The pain was too intense.

As I cried and whimpered, I was walking with difficulty. Mom was standing at the bottom of the stairs, and I looked over at Princess who had the same deceitful look. She was always creating drama, and she never went into the bathroom. I recognized this was another one of their many plots to strike at my self-worth!

Once everyone was gone, I attempted to take a hot bubble bath. Big Mistake: the hot water and soap irritated me which intensified the pain. Days later, while playing over a friend's house, I was having pain in my vagina. The pain was so intense.

I cried and complained about my hostile environment. I told her that I had been molested by my sister and teenage cousin. She was flabbergasted. We made a pinkie promise that she swore to keep it a secret.

Fast forward…

Everyone was looking forward to summer break. Mua, 'mysterious child' and my two younger cousins came to visit and I was so glad to see them. They stayed at Aunt Ellen's house on the northside, so I went over to spend some time with them.

There was animosity with 'mysterious child' and Cousin Dawg who is Aunt Ellen's youngest child.

We all went outside to play when Cousin Dawg motioned for us to come to the playground. Once we were in arm's reach, he grabbed 'mysterious child.'

As she was kicking, cussing, and fighting he pinned her between his legs. He then took her strings out of her shoes & tied her to the merry go round. He spun it in full force, and she flew off, hurting herself. Her hands, arms and legs were bruised and bleeding. She was limping and crying as she walked to auntie's house.

***

Mua left to go home after a few weeks and took my cousins with her. I enjoyed spending quality time with them.

'Mysterious child' got to stay and I was happy because I was looking forward to playing with my younger sister. I thought, "It's going to be different and exciting having her in the same house."

Since she always lived with Mua, we never bonded as sisters. With her living in Sacramento California summer break was the only chance for her to visit Ohio.

'Mysterious child' was happy to stay in Ohio without Mua. She knew she would be able to run amuck with us.

We were planning on hanging out at the recreation center because we could have lots of fun there. There would be kids inside playing basketball, ping pong, hide and seek or doing arts and crafts.

Outside, several children were enjoying the sun and water in the splash pad. There was a small fee to enjoy all the amenities. The facilitator knew each family who was represented. She would walk through the building calling out your last name if you were not in good standing. She would ask you to leave until your dues were paid. However, if you brought her some fish, she would allow you to stay.

Everyone knew she loved fish.

If it was your unlucky day, you knew the drill. Hurry to the back door and someone will allow you back in.

***

Princess and I were looking forward to being cheerleaders for the Eastside Vikings. I was excited and looking forward to cheering. The coach's wife, several of the girls and myself went door to door soliciting donations to pay for our uniforms. After several days of canvassing, everyone was anticipating being on the cheer squad.

I was outside playing when I saw Ms. Coach drive up in her van. She was a heavy lady so most of the time she would pull up and honk. I heard her honk and ignored it since Mom had already said I could not be on the squad. Princess went out of the house and turned in her donation envelope.

Minutes later, Princess called me to come to the van. It was apparent by her stupid grin that she had already told her what Mom said. Now I am hurting and crying on the inside. Ms. Coach asked me if I collected donations. Without reiterating what Mom instructed. I said, "Yes."

She then said I am here to pick up the money. I went into the house to tell Mom. She looked at me without saying anything. I stood there waiting for Mom to reply. After about five minutes, Ms. Coach began honking the horn to get my attention. A few choice words later, I went to the car.

Once she saw I didn't have the money. The look on her face changed as she said that she would 'call the police' to get the money that was collected. I hurried to relay the information. Mom didn't want any police contact, so she grudgingly gave me the money, cussing me out at the same time. I was called stupid, nappy head and bald headed. She told me, "The sight of you disgusts me."

I could not understand why Mom would humiliate me. After all she never gave me a valid reason why she changed her mind about not letting me cheer. All I knew was that she was always striking my self-esteem.

A few days later after cheerleading practice, Princess and her posse were late getting home. One of the girl's moms was alarmed by her daughter not being home. Ms. Mom was worried half to death, so she went to check on her.

When she got to the school, no one was there. All the cars were gone so she rode up the hill to the top of the field and no one was there. She franticly hurried back home to see if she had returned. When she saw that she wasn't back. She began to pace the floor and explained how she was reluctant to allow her daughter to walk home.

Dust dark was approaching, and the streetlights would be coming on shortly; this raised her fear. By now, every concerned mother was panicking and checking on their kids; the scene had gotten chaotic.

Our mom was in the house passed out on the couch.

The police were called, they took a report and left. Ms. Girlfriend picked us up for the weekend. As we raced to the car, Princess got there first and got in the front seat. I told her it was my turn to sit shotgun and she looked at me and rolled her eyes. She sat there and ignored me as always.

Ms. Girlfriend reiterated what I said. "Princess it *is* Kandie's turn."

Princess was pissed off because she was used to getting her way. She said, "**But** Kandie…"

Ms. Girlfriend interrupted, "It's Kandie's turn."

As she was getting in the backseat, she rolled her eyes at us. Once she and Blaze were seated, she started kicking me under the seat. I politely asked her to stop. When she refused Blaze hit her. I was glad they spoke up...

THATS LOVE!

She was well behaved and silent for the rest of the ride. Ms. Girlfriend was always fair. When we arrived at their house, she was crying and ran to tell Dad. Dad jumped down Blaze's back and told me to quit being a tattle tale. We all tried to tell him what happened, but he didn't care. He kept saying to Blaze, "You don't have any kids and you better keep your hands to yourself."

She stood there grinning as usual. She never got reprimanded and he knew she was lying as usual.

***

Mr. Butler was Mom's new man. He lived with us

and he appeared to be happy; we all liked him. He was always laughing and interacting with everyone.

After a long day of work, he would pick up Mom's slack. This enabled her to do what she wanted so she continued to bloom into a social butterfly.

One pretty spring day after school, Mom wasn't home. Mr. Butler was there cooking and cleaning her bedroom. I asked him where Mom was. He said, "In the hospital."

Scratching my head... in the hospital?

A few days later she came home with a newborn baby girl. I was shocked! I was thinking, "Who's baby is this and what is going on?"

Seeing the twinkles in mom and Mr. Butler's eyes told the story. Their eyes were magnetic, and their smiles were priceless. It was clear who the happy parents were.

She was dressed in a bright pink outfit, with a hat and

hand booties to match. All bundled up in a white receiving blanket with bright pink lace. They named her Precious and it fit her. She was their rainbow bright, their light skinned love child.

I was feeling lost; Mom had another baby.

I was clueless trying to find out what was going on. I sat on the sofa hoping to get some clarity. Mom had several visitors, and each of them had a perplexed look on their face.

Of course, this would be the time when Mom would say, "Princess you and Kandie can go to your bedroom, there are no kids down here."

As I walked towards the stairs, Princess sat there pretending she didn't hear Mom and mumbling. She didn't want to go upstairs, so she turned and blurted out to me, "Quit following me!" She was implying that the only reason she must go upstairs is because I decided to stay down there. I agreed with her.

My parents always talked about kids staying in their place. They never made her stay in her place.

It was CUTE to THEM!

After confiding in a friend, I shared my innermost thoughts and feelings about how my mom and siblings were treating me. She was speechless. Once she gathered her thoughts, she began to tell me about God as I was looking upside her head. This was not the response I was looking for.

After she finished, she invited me to attend church with her the following Sunday. I often thought about going to church when I watched many children from my bedroom window for several years as the bus arrived and departed. I noticed a difference in their demeanor when they returned. They appeared to be carefree, as if they had no problems or worries about anything.

Needless to say, my siblings nor I attended.

Being traumatized and violated at an earlier age, I was filled with rage. I needed love, prayer, and God to heal my broken heart. Mr. Husband gave it his all which was commendable, yet the man who adored me never spoke a word. After seeing me a few times he passed away.

***

During school pictures, the photographer mistook me for a boy. I was devastated and embarrassed and I couldn't wait for school to be over. I hurried home to tell Mom and her response was, "Well you do look like a boy."

I was crying and thinking, "You don't comb my hair; you made me look like this. I have a short afro with no hair accessories or earrings."

What is more hurtful is she had a neighbor do Princess' hair, but not mine.

Later that evening, she came into my bedroom and

gave me a wig. I looked up at her in disbelief. She said, "Wear it or look like a boy."

I fought back tears.

I tried to suck it up, but it was too much for me. The fluttering in my heart made it difficult to contain myself. I let out a loud cry as she put it on my head and walked away.

I got in my bed and put my head under the cover as I cried myself to sleep. When I woke up, I hurried to the bathroom. As I passed the mirror, you can imagine my pain. Once I finished, I returned to my bedroom to see an empty wig head sitting on my dresser.

***

That Saturday morning after the 'Fat Albert Cartoon' went off, Eric, Bobby, Lyda, Pookie and me were congregated outside by the chain petition. Wesley walked up and threatened to pull off my wig and I dared him.

He did it.

As everyone is looking and trying to break it up. One of the village mothers was yelling from inside her screen door, "Let her go!! He needs his butt beat!! He had no right to pull off her wig."

I was kicking and punching him with all my might. When it was over, someone handed me my wig. I put it on crooked and hurried home.

When I got home, I went straight to the bathroom crying as I looked in the mirror at the ugly crooked wig that was wreaking havoc.

"Havoc means to cause considerable confusion or damage."

This fight was the gossip for weeks to come. Getting your butt beat by a girl. Not long afterwards, his home boy Bobby wanted to challenge me. Back then if you wanted to fight someone, the instigators would put a stick on your shoulder and if your opponent knocked it off it was war.

However, I was different when you got within arm's reach. I would punch you as hard as I could in the face with my hard right hand. I was full of rage. The rest is His-story.

Yea! He felt stupid.

I beat his butt and his friend was there to witness. I was at my breaking point and didn't know my strength. The rage that had been brewing inside of me had overflown. With the constant abuse from Mom and my siblings, I refused to take any form of abuse from the streets.

I hurried home reluctant to tell her about what happened. As I entered the house, I accidentally slammed the door. It was evident I was upset. Mom yelled, "What's your problem slamming my door?"

I told her I got in a fight with another boy. Needless to say, it never phased her, her only concern was, "Did you beat his BUTT?" She always promoted violence.

I was upset by her reaction: she didn't care. Yes, kids can be cruel and living in that type of environment comes with the territory. That does not negate the fact that as kids we look to our parents to love, protect, and provide.

I dashed past her to go to my bedroom. I sat in there all alone sobbing and thinking, "Mom just doesn't care about me."

At that moment, I realized it was not if I won or lost. It hurt me to my core knowing my mother would be spiteful towards me. There was never any love when it came to Kandie.

This is what my fights have been about: me standing up for myself. I recognized it was another one of her many tactics to strike at my self-esteem with hopes of destroying my self-worth.

As my mom, she never tried to rectify the situation and she never asked any questions. Not to mention having Princess' hair styled religiously gave her bragging rights which intensified my pain. The love she has for Princess is priceless. I was tired of feeling unloved and unworthy!

***

I laid there looking at the moon and cried myself to sleep.

Before long, I was awakened by the sounds of rain hitting the window. As I walked towards the window, I could hear the wind whistling. The house was quiet and still, and I was home alone once again.

Once the rain stopped, I went outside where everyone was assembled and eager to talk about the fight. It was hilarious hearing everyone laughing and telling their views. Shortly afterward it began to rain so we decided to go home. As I walked home, I remember thanking God for no one mentioning that ugly wig. Boy that was a big relief!

I remember thinking it was *not* a good sight. What mother would do that? I thought to myself, "I prefer for my hair to be uncombed because that was my norm. I'm not wearing that wig again."

I walked into the kitchen and took the straightening comb out the drawer and began pressing my hair. Shortly afterwards, Basil came home and asked me, "What is that smell?"

Before I could answer, he replied, "It smells like wet, burnt hair. What are you doing girl? You better turn off that stove."

I turned off the stove and went to my bedroom. I stood in front of the mirror frustrated and crying.

Basil is eight years my senior and a young man who was acting as an aspiring barber. He would give his friends a debonair look. Later that day, his best friend Duck came by to get a haircut. He said, "Man I will take care of you after I give Kandie a blowout."

Although I was thankful it looked nice, I didn't like it! I had a mini afro; I had short hair which society considered a 'bald head.' I didn't want to look like that. I wanted my ears pierced and my hair combed with some pretty hair barrettes and ribbons.

After exhausting all options, I was forced to learn how to comb my own hair. I went into my bedroom and before long, I was Frenching my hair. Although I had done it a few times on my baby doll. I was proud of how well I did. The parts were crooked, but anything was better than that '227' looking wig.

When I was done, I put some colorful barrettes on. I looked and felt pretty as I left the room to show off my artwork and new look. Princess started yelling, "Take off my barrettes." Mom yelled up the stairs don't mess with her stuff. After I finished crying, I took off Princess's barrettes and went outside to catch some lightning bugs to emulate earrings.

"There are people whose plotted against you who are around today, still wondering, "How the HELL did you survive??"

— John Bryant

***

I was looking forward to my big day when I planned to go to church. I asked Mom if she could French braid or hot comb my hair like she did Princess's and pierce my ears. She said angrily, "Your short nappy hair makes my hands cramp. I had to let your ears close due to keloids."

She was always mean.

Mr. Butler hot combed my hair. It was awkward getting my hair done by a man although I never complained. It made me feel loved to know he cared.

After a long atrocious week, I was looking forward to receiving what God had in store for me and Saturday night was longer than usual. Sunday morning, I arrived at my friend's house feeling anxious.

After boarding the bus, I sat there quietly gazing out the window enjoying the scenery. When we finally arrived, everyone was excited and eager to get off the bus. My anxiety was at an all-time high. I didn't know what to do and the feeling was awkward. Walking through the church doors was a start to what was to come.

I felt a sense of peace being in God's presence. With the Holy Spirit at work, my mind shifted, as the ushers greeted me with a big inviting smile and warm embrace.

During the service, I felt like all eyes were on me. I sat there with my head hung down using my peripheral vision to gauge my surroundings. I refused to stand when they said, "First time visitors please stand."

My friend and others looked at me and I pretended not to see them. She then nudged me to stand, and I nudged her back to stop.

The sermon was on family and unity. Although I could not fully articulate the message, my mind and thoughts were all over the place. More so because I hadn't been in church since Mua left.

At the end of the sermon, the pastor said that Easter Sunday would be the next baptismal. I was thinking about it but was apprehensive since I didn't fully understand the benefits.

After service, many parishioners were fellowshipping in small groups. On the way home Tina explained she was planning to be baptized and suggested I do so as well. I told her how I felt about the sermon and accused her of telling my business, assuming that was why everyone was looking at me. When we arrived at our bus stop, I hurried off the bus and went home without saying goodbye; I was mad.

As I walked home, I hung my head in despair feeling as though my trust had been violated once again and in fear of Princess knowing I had talked about the family business. I must mention it had nothing to do with her interceding on my behalf. This could have been ammunition for her to tell Mom since she mimicked Mom's behavior.

She was jealous and looking for a reason to be nasty towards me. I was in fear of her confiding in her older sisters since she would go over to their house. She always gravitated to the older crowd.

***

A few days later, I was outside on the porch playing jacks. When Tina came by, her appearance made me livid, and it was evident in my behavior. She spoke to me, and I ignored her. She spoke again thinking I didn't hear her. I proceeded to look up at her rolling my eyes.

At that moment, she knew I was upset. She began to reassure me she never shared my business, and we made the pinkie promise.

As she was proclaiming her innocence the Holy Spirit chastised me again, reiterating what the pastor spoke. "Trust God He is **INTENTIONAL**; He sees and knows everything. God can and will do all things but fail you."

MISTAKES ARE MADE FOR *a reason*

***

Easter Sunday finally arrived, and I was looking forward to a new beginning. I was awakened by the bright light from the sun shining through the window. I hurried to get dressed and tried not to wake Princess.

I went downstairs and Mom was the only one awake. She was sitting on the sofa smoking a cigarette, so she walked me to the door. As I exited the house I said, "Bye Mom."

She replied, "Um don't be down there talking about my business."

The same scenario, different day.

As I hurried to Tina's house, I saw other kids and their families dressed in their Sunday best. Everyone was dressed in beautiful pastel Easter colors leaving for church.

I was looking forward to publicly inviting Jesus Christ into my heart.

—Tonya "Kandie" Thomas

As Pastor Hope acknowledged my entrance, I entered the baptismal pool and felt light on my feet. As he read the confession of faith and dunked me under water, it was surreal. The feeling was mind blowing, something I have never been able to articulate.

Once it was done, I recalled thinking, "This is all I had to do?"

Now God is going to fight all my battles. As I exited the water the weight shifted.

GLORY!

CHAPTER 5:

Illigetimate Children

Mom never took the time to embrace motherhood. Due to her lack of LOVE and consideration for her unborn children she never had any prenatal care.

"Prenatal care is when you get checkups from a doctor, nurse, or midwife throughout your pregnancy. It helps to keep you and your future baby healthy. During pregnancy women should not use tobacco, alcohol, marijuana, illegal drugs, or prescription medicine for nonmedical reasons."

Mom continued smoking cigarettes, drank alcohol, and partied which had a profound effect on each of her children, either mentally or physically.

"Avoiding these substances and getting regular prenatal care are important to having a healthy

pregnancy and healthy baby. A woman should never have a baby out of obligation.

There are too many methods of birth control as well as adoption and abortion. Whatever the case may be, no child deserves to be mistreated. Depending on where you live, there is a safe haven where you can drop the baby off clean and unharmed at the local hospitals and fire stations within seventy-two hours after giving birth, anonymously.

I assume my mom's state of mind was that she gave birth to a damn baby girl who she should have aborted. I was not her husband's child and if her marriage had a chance, it was over when she had me.

"Abortion is the deliberate termination of human pregnancy. The main causes for an abortion are financial reasons, not the right time for a baby,

partner related reasons, needs to focus on other children, or a new baby will interfere with future opportunities. One may not be emotionally or mentally prepared, health related reasons, or desires a better life for the baby then they can provide."

She never showed me any love or affection. The mere mention of my name or the site of seeing me sent her blood boiling. She would make vulgar comments and or roll her eyes at me.

<u>Mom</u> had unprotected sex. This was a MISTAKE.

Although a mistake, it is how I was conceived. It became clear, I was a product of an adulterous affair and viewed as a 'mistake.' This explained why my father was absent.

However, I should not have been made to *feel* like I am a **MISTAKE** or the cause for her failed marriage. Not to mention two and half years later Mom was in the same situation having another illegitimate baby girl 'mysterious child' who she didn't want; we are two years apart in age.

I didn't know she was my sister for many years. Mua came to visit Mom and to her dismay there were seven crying, frightened, hungry kids ranging from ages newborn to ten years old: home alone.

From that day forward, she lived with Mua. This explained who the man was and why she looked at us harshly. However, 'mysterious child' was blessed to have a loving supportive father, grandmother and aunt who loved her unconditionally.

She was always easily influenced and had an ungrateful spirit. She was known for wrongdoing and would steal anything that was not nailed down.

One day, a neighbor was moving out and we were helping them by taking boxes to the moving truck. She stayed behind, stole a popsicle, and ate it. When she saw us coming, she threw the remains under the couch. She and I are cordial for the most part.

Precious is the third illegitimate child, and we had a cool bond. For many years while Mom was preoccupied with her addiction, I had to mother my three youngest siblings. Precious, Martina, and Pear. She viewed me as her big sister, and I was always there for her.

She got pregnant with her first child at fourteen years old and needed financial and sisterly advice. Mom was obviously not in the right state of mind, and they were at odds. She lived with me until they were able to rectify their differences.

One day during a family gathering, she spat in my daughter's face and turned to me and said, "My mom HATES YOU!"

It was evident that Mom had scored again.

Fifteen months later, it was the same situation. Mom had another girl: Martina, her ninth child. Now she has four sons and five daughters, not to mention two more heads to comb.

Even though Martina's hair was shorter than mine and very coarse, she did their hair gracefully and never complained about her fingers cramping.

***

Martina and I have a big sister-little sister relationship. As a kid, she loved the way I braided her hair with colorful beads. We have always respected each other's thoughts and views.

She was always getting in trouble and fighting with Mom. She was smoking, drinking, and running away from home so Mom put her in juvenile hall. Needless to say, Mom would sneak to visit her regularly. She would take three city buses and bring her snacks, food, and cigarettes. I never understood the logic. More so, Mom always had a hidden agenda.

***

At thirteen years old, she gave birth to her first child. Princess and I were there with her as big sisters should have been, but Mom refused to come.

A few months prior, Martina had the courage to speak life into our dead sibling relationship and owned her shortcomings. I thank God for all the provisions He made in her life.

She explained to me how she 'loved and admired' me as her big sister and I was her favorite. As she fought back tears, she attempted to explain how Mom had been a major influence on each of their relationships with **ME**.

She said, "It saddened me to know Mom has deleted you KANDIE! Princess is so darn messy with her jealousy BUTT…" Wiping her eyes, she hugged me and said, "Quit trying to make amends, you better not say another speech!"

She was referring to our family because we had lost several family members in a short span. I would always have a word of encouragement.

Thanks LIL SIS, my "FAVORITE" your encouraging words propelled ME!!

"Your character is a projection of who you are."

—Tonya "Kandie" Thomas

***

One very cold December morning, I woke up feeling colder than usual. I stared out the window watching the snowflakes falling. Curious to see how much snow had fallen, I walked over to look outside. Once the window was opened, I grabbed an icicle. After eating it, I went downstairs.

Mom was leaning over the kitchen sink washing dishes. When she noticed my presence, she said, "Go to Ms. Neighbor's house." I stood there waiting for her to complete her sentence, but she repeated softly, looked with authority, and said, "Go!"

I hurried up the street, looked back and Mom was coming out of the house. It was apparent Ms. Neighbor was aware because she was on standby.

As I knocked on her door, she hurried out the door carrying her purse and car keys. She walked past me and met Mom near her car.

Later that day, I was outside playing in the snow. We made angels and a snowman. While we were making a snowman, a friend said, "Your mom had another baby."

I am looking at him like, "What are you talking about? I just saw my mom."

He repeated, "Your mom had a baby boy!"

146

I stood there speechless.

I was thinking, "Mom had another baby. This is her tenth child, another son."

The family has grown to five boys and five girls. He is the last of the Thomas's. He was spoiled and bad as all outdoors! He would cuss like Mom and there were no consequences. He would tell you to suck his d*** or call you a B****. Mom was preoccupied with her own issues, so she never took the time to police him. If you told Mom about his behavior, her solution was, "Leave him alone and he won't disrespect you."

After disrespecting me a time or two, we never had any more issues. I pride myself on being a big sister and a role model. I taught him how to ride a bike.

When he was in high school, and needed support, he would call me crying. His girlfriend Tracy would bring him over and I would make his favorite meal homemade burritos and Mexican rice with refried beans or homemade Chinese food.

A few years ago, I spoke to him and he didn't respond. I asked him if there was an issue with him and he said, "No, but Mom and Princess get mad when I talk to you."

I didn't want to be in the middle of the mess, so I just don't talk to you.

CHAPTER 6:

Lack Of Parenting

Winter was approaching, so Mom took Princess and I to Hill's Department Store at McGuffey Mall. We needed new shoes and coats.

Once we were in the store, we went to the shoe department. After trying on several pairs of shoes, we found the perfect fit: a pair of black quarter top boots. When I put them on, Mom said to walk up the aisle and come back, then she asked how they felt. I told her they felt good, and I liked them. As I was standing there admiring my new shoes and thanking Mom for being so nice, I looked up at Princess and she was wearing the exact coat that I wanted. It was. a lavender puff Eskimo coat; along with her signature deceitful grin.

After finding the right size, Mom asked, "How does it feel? Stretch your arms."

This was the latest style, and I had my eyes on it. The zip out hood was awesome to keep the blizzard cold winter weather chill off my face. As Mom zipped up my coat, she said, "Follow Princess."

As I looked at her to reassure myself, I heard her clearly repeat herself, "FOLLOW PRINCESS! Do you want new shoes and a coat?"

I said, "Yes Mom."

Princess was standing at the end of the aisle closer to the exit. As I walked toward her, Mom was going in the opposite direction. Upon approaching the front door, an older man cut off my path and asked me to come with him. As I looked clueless to what was happening, I could see Mom looking at me rolling her eyes while Princess took off running across the parking lot to the car.

As I walked to the back office with the man, there was a lady sitting there. I couldn't understand what was going on. Once we entered the office, the man left. I sat down in the chair where I could see my old shoes on display. The lady introduced herself and explained why I was there. I looked at her, not fully understanding what she meant by 'SHOPLIFTING!'

She then said you stole those shoes and coat. I started crying thinking, "My mom bought these for me."

She asked me who the people were shopping with me. I told her about my sister and mother. As I began crying out of control, she reassured me It was not my fault because she had witnessed everything on the security surveillance camera.

Her statement got my immediate attention.

She continued to ask me questions like, "How old are you? Have you done this before?"

The man had come back and he walked over and whispered in the lady's ear. When he was finished, he stood by the door. As I sat there with my head hung low and crying, no one said a word. I was waiting and expecting Mom to rescue me because after all, this was her doing. We sat there for what seemed like forever and my mom never came. Suddenly Uncle Midnight entered the room, and it was apparent he had been drinking because he was loud with slurring speech. He looked over at me as his eyes were fixated on my old torn up shoes on display.

As he stood there trying to figure out what was going on, being under the influence of alcohol it was difficult for him to grasp. He stood in the doorway hanging his head and trying to hold his balance. The man explained to him that I had stolen a coat and pair of boots. He said I would be prosecuted, would have to go to court and he needed his signature.

He was reluctant to sign the waiver.

At that moment, he looked like a deer in the headlights. His posture straightened up as he told him, "I will be right back."

I looked up as he walked out of the room hoping he wouldn't abandon me as well. Once he left, I began giving the situation more thought. His bewildered demeanor spoke volumes and I was sure he was not a part of the scam.

It was hilarious seeing how his demeanor changed in a flash. I surmised how he must have been thinking walking back to the car, "My niece got caught stealing and my sister brought her."

While we were waiting and anticipating for Mom to come and rescue me, the lady asked me to take off the stolen items. I walked over to retrieve my old shoes from the shelf.

A short time later, Uncle Midnight returned bright eyes and bushy tail without Mom. He stopped in the doorway and adjusted his belt as he apologized for my behavior. I looked up in disbelief as he was placing the blame on me. He grudgingly signed the papers to attend court.

As we quietly left the store, he was walking so fast I could not keep up with him. I felt angry and degraded knowing Mom made me steal and had the audacity to leave me.

Once we got to the car, Princess and Mom were quieter than a church house mouse. Then Princess began antagonizing me by zipping and unzipping her new coat and tying and untying her new boots.

As we continued home, it was evident Mom was upset with me. Princess knew how to get Mom's attention, so she began thanking Mom for the new things; Mom ignored her.

After Princess continued to insist on getting Mom's attention by tapping on her shoulder and talking louder than the radio, Mom attempted to get her to shut up. When she didn't, Uncle Midnight told Mom, "You didn't tell me that was the plan. You know you are wrong for having me to take you to boost with those kids."

He told her over and over how it pissed him off but

she shrugged it off. He told her, "Kandie has been needing some new shoes."

She said, "That's her fault."

He was outraged.

He then said, "Winter is coming, and her toes are hanging out of those shoes."

Mom said, "Those are her damn feet, she should have listened!!"

As I am crying, Princess continues her shenanigans.

Mom scrutinized me by yelling, "You didn't do what I told you. I told you to follow Princess, that's your DAMN fault!! Now you don't have any boots or a coat."

As I sat there crying, she felt no pity. I remember thinking to myself, "Why is Mom so cruel? Why did she take me to steal?"

She angrily ordered me, "Shut up before I give you something to cry about."

Hearing those words was devastating!

I sucked up my tears and muffled my cries thinking they must have done this a time or two, like mother like daughter. Mom had so much malice in her heart when it came to me.

Once we made it home, I went straight to my bedroom and my rage towards her multiplied. I didn't want to hear Mom's mouth or watch Princess model her new boots and coat. Princess took the liberty to model from the living room to upstairs inside our bedroom and back downstairs again until each brother acknowledged her presence.

I closed the bedroom door. All I could hear was, "THATS CUTE!"

Feeling dejected, I buried my head in my pillow to

block them out. Needless to say, no one asked about me.

A few hours later, I awakened. As I sat on the end of my bed stretching, I turned to look at my old jacket lying on my bed. Princess had taken it off the hanger to put her new coat on it.

She always antagonized me.

Her and Mom's goal was to destroy me any way possible. I turned over to stretch the other way. I noticed she placed her new shoes on the dresser.

Now THATS CUTE!

Whenever I complained about being cold, she often reminded me, "It's your fault, and you will learn how to listen. I said follow **Princess,** I didn't tell you to go with no DAMN man!!"

I didn't get any boots or a winter coat that year.

MISTAKES ARE MADE FOR *a reason*

***

Precious and I were in the bedroom lying on the bed and Mr. Butler would check on us periodically. I was upset at Mom for not allowing me to cheer and I always wondered why she never told me the reason I could not cheer.

The door opened and I pretended to be asleep. Princess and her posse entered along with the one girl whose mother was concerned she was not home yet.

Precious was asleep and they were talking about the eventful day that brewed. They were laughing and discussing how they took their fast butts to the Plaza View and the Victory Apartments without permission. This was normal after cheer practice.

The girl who was not in attendance wanted to go. Her mom was always hands on and didn't allow her kids out of her sight. She even worked at the school and was president on the PTA Board. They concocted a big lie to keep from getting in trouble.

TONYA "KANDIE" THOMAS

Talk about deceitful!

I am willing to bet Princess masterminded it. I told Mom what I heard, and she didn't even seem surprised. She responded, "You are always tattle telling."

A few weeks later, Princess ran away from home. Mom said, "She was smelling herself."

Yes, she became a preteen hanging with older women courting, smoking, drinking, and hanging out in the Plaza View, Victory Apartments, and the Ellison Motel. I would see her around the Brooks playing and being fast as usual.

Mom called the police and as she was talking to the officer, Princess walked by abruptly to evade the police. Mom was screaming and pleading with her to come home.

Biker walked up and called her name and that was when she surrendered. They always had a close bond and she returned home like nothing ever happened.

That was cute.

There were never any consequences for her actions. She did not interact with us because she was too advanced for us kids. She lied about her age and was good at looking like she was older than thirteen. She had been engaging in adult activities for quite some time.

***

One hot muggy day, I was sitting on the front porch playing with jacks when Princess and Mom walked past me. I looked up to see a deceitful smug look on Princess' face while Mom talked trash with a cigarette in the corner of her mouth and a beer in her hand.

Not a pretty site.

When they started down the sidewalk, Mom was

confrontational saying, "She better stay out of my business."

I knew trouble had escalated, so I gathered my belongings and followed them. The neighbor who Mom was going to confront was sitting on her porch with her children. Mom called her over when she got close. Mom hit her in her face and told her not to ever talk about her business again.

Princess and her friends took the liberty to jump in, kicking and hitting the lady. Princess threw Mom's beer on her during the fight.

On the way back home, Mom told her, "Don't ever waste my beer on a dirty nasty tramp like that ever again!"

As I listened carefully, I attempted to find out what was said, but everyone was talking about the fight. I agreed, it was funny, but I was more concerned about what she said that upset Mom.

Mom and Princess never spoke about the reason for the fight. Days later I heard a neighbor talking about the fight so I listened intensely hoping she would repeat the gossip. She stated it was rumored that Princess was seen with Mom at the local gynecologist office having a procedure done. Now I am thinking, "What procedure? Is she okay?"

I wouldn't dare ask any questions.

Although Princess was only nine months older than me, I was doing age-appropriate stuff. The disconnect was obvious and not too many people knew we were so close in age. But we were complete opposites, and we all have our own issues.

Basil was chilled, that was his way of dealing with it. He channeled his pain differently.

Donald (RIP) needed emergency professional counseling. He was always mean; he put me in the deep freezer for no apparent reason.

Biker had difficulty sleeping due to adenoids and a tied tongue.

Blaze had a learning disability.

Princess was a brat in every sense of the word.

'Mysterious child' was deprived of love which caused her to misbehave.

Precious was born with a birth defect. Her umbilical cord was wrapped around her hand and hindered the growth of two fingers.

Mom refused to seek medical care due to pride.

Martina had resentment and some anger issues towards Mom; I surmise since finding a dead body in the woods.

Pear had some health issues as a baby which required him to have a spinal tap. As a toddler, Mom neglected to have him immunized and he started having issues with his legs and joints.

MISTAKES ARE MADE FOR *a reason*

***

With summer coming to an end, it was clear that Mua missed 'mysterious child,' so she would call every day. Mua was getting concerned about 'mysterious child' going home to California in time for school. Mom reassured her that she would have her home in time.

One grim evening, Mom dropped her three oldest daughters ages 9, 12, and 13 off at the trailway bus station with two bologna sandwiches, a couple pieces of fruit five dollars and a one-way ticket to California. We were on our way to Sacramento California roughly 2,500 miles away which was a three day trip with two layovers and bus changes.

My first thoughts were that I would get peace of mind and a sense of relief, and I'd be free from that hell hole we called home. As the night grew long, I could not believe we were on our way to California.

Although I was happy to be leaving, I must admit I was frightened half to death. I sat there in fear as I stared out the window. As the night grew long, the fear became more intense. I could not believe Mom put her three minor daughters on a bus all alone.

I sat there with my head buried as I quietly cried myself to sleep. Several hours later, I was awakened by the bus driver abruptly pulling over to the side of a dark, lonely, deserted highway.

Once the bus stopped, the driver proceeded to the back of the bus saying he smelled something burning. As the other passengers and I looked to see what was going on, I noticed both my sisters were seated at the back of the bus in the smoking area. This was in the late 70's when you were allowed to smoke in the back three rows.

A white man with long greasy hair was laughing saying, "Thank you for the hair cut youngster."

'Mysterious child' had set his hair on fire.

The driver asked them, "Where are your parents and where are you all going? Why are you two smoking?"

They answered the questions honestly and his reply was, "Wow!" as he scratched his head. "Why are you two smoking?"

Before they could answer, he shook his head in disbelief. He ordered them to get in their original seats and stay. Once they were seated, we continued down the lonely dark highway, keeping his eyes on them. They sat there trying to be on their best behavior.

Once we laid over in Chicago, they took off running down the street with other passengers to get some soul food. I sat there with our luggage, and a couple who were traveling to California.

Within twenty-four hours, I got food poisoning from eating the stale sandwiches. The abdominal pain was bothersome and the next two days were miserable.

The bad abdominal cramps caused me to vomit and have diarrhea.

When we arrived, I was weak, sore, and drained as the bus pulled into the depot. Seeing Mua and her best friend standing there with open arms and a big smile melted my heart.

That was love.

It was evident she missed us but they greeted us with a big hug. Precious and 'mysterious child' told Mua that I had been sick. Not because they were concerned but because that was their way of deflecting.

Mua immediately started asking questions and doctoring on me, something Mom had never done. She was always loving and nurturing, unlike Mom.

On the ride home, we stopped at the store to get a 7up for my upset stomach. As we drove down Broadway, I was captivated by the modern look and all the fruit and pine trees. The weather was nice and everything looked different. It was breathtaking coming to a beautiful, clean, paved street. It was a culture shock coming from a small town to a big city.

 Mua lived in the Oak Park neighborhood, in a white house with a big backyard and a two-story garage. Her best friend lived across the street, and she would always say, "You gals better appreciate Ruby."

The family next door to her shared the same first cousins. My uncle and their aunt were married. We became good friends and I spent a lot of time over there. Also, Brenda Morrison and her sisters would spend a lot of time at their grandparents' home down the street and we became good friends.

Over the next few days, each of my uncles would come over. They each had the same thoughts and reactions to Mom sending us cross country all alone for Mua to take on the responsibility to care for Princess and myself. It angered them to know their elderly Mom was forced to pick up her slack. Not to mention she was already raising my two minor cousins who were barely school age and my younger sister 'mysterious child.'

Uncle Pound (RIP) would come over daily and Mua would always make him a peanut butter and jelly sandwich. He didn't say much but he always gave me an uneasy look. It was obvious why he was upset.

Everyone had the same reaction. They were angry at their sister who is my mother, however I got punished.

One day, I was hungry, and he told me to eat a P and J sandwich or have some top ramen because 'Doc' is not cooking today. I sat on the sofa pouting and Princess lied and said I flipped him off.

Without even asking, he snatched me up, put me in a footlocker (suitcase) and closed it while he was sitting on top. They were laughing as I cried to the top of my lungs.

***

Uncle Smooth lived down the street in the fairgrounds with his girlfriend and daughter. Often, he would come over and a time or two, he allowed me to go to his house to swim.

They had several big community pools and he always took Princess with him. When I would ask to go, he would make an excuse. He was mad because I told Mua he was allowing her to smoke weed with him.

"Respect is earned not given."

Tonya Kandie Thomas

Uncle Relo (RIP) called, and Mua told him we were there. He immediately came over and always spoke

his mind out of love. After he finished blessing Mom out, he then focused his attention on my appearance.

He said, "Damn your momma sent you looking like that Kandie? She could have braided your hair."

Although I didn't appreciate the derogatory remarks, I felt loved. When he heard about me getting food poisoning, he lost it. The next day he came and took me to Kmart to get new clothes and shoes.

Mua made me an appointment to get my hair pressed and curled at the beauty salon on Stockton Blvd.

After getting my hair done, we picked up a pizza across the street.

Those were fun times. Uncle Goldie is mom's baby brother, and he still lives at home. He had a big German Shepherd dog in the backyard I was afraid of, so I never went back there by myself. He was glad to see us and upset for obvious reasons.

The love he displayed was epic.

It was breathtaking for him to know his three young nieces traveled all alone. Everything he was saying, I totally agreed with. His thoughts were the same as mine during the long grim bus ride across the country. Once he contained himself there was a warm embrace.

***

When the weekend arrived, Auntie Diva came to visit. I was glad to see her, and she was happy to see us, yet livid at the same time. She was visibly upset that Mom allowed us to travel by ourselves. She kept repeating, "Why would she do that? What's her problem?"

When she pulled herself together, I asked her to pierce my ears. She responded, "Your momma hasn't gotten your ears pierced?"

I told her what Mom said that Aunt Diva had pierced my ears when I was a baby, and she was forced to allow my ears to close due to sores and keloids. She said, "Your mom is a liar!" Further examination confirmed my ears had never been pierced.

Later that day, Auntie Diva got two wooden clothespins, a cube of ice, and a needle and thread. After numbing my ears, I got two holes in each ear and Princess got one. Since she had previously had her ears pierced, she had to get *hers* done also.

OF COURSE, she is the PRINCESS!

***

I was starting to feel better about myself. I received new clothes, shoes, my hair was done and my ears were pierced....

NOW THATS CUTE!

All their concerns were valid. The love each of them displayed warmed my heart. The problem I had was having to continue to hear about Mom's irresponsible behaviors and ENDURE Princess' vindictive and conniving ways.

***

Uncle Black came to take us to visit my Aunt Bea who lived in the red brick apartments by the cemetery. It was creepy seeing the cemetery across from the apartments.

Once we arrived, Uncle Black opened his car hood to check his fluids. As 'mysterious child' and my cousins went into the house. Princess and I were playing and talking under the shade tree. We both agreed we didn't want to go in the house due to the pungent smell.

Uncle Black looked over at us and suggested we go into the house and get out of the hot sun. Princess and I looked at each other and she told him what we both agreed on, but saying *I* said it! She is a habitual liar and a troublemaker.

It pissed him off.

He grabbed me as he pulled out the hot dip stick from under the hood of his car and hit me a few times across my stomach. I am crying telling him Princess said it too, but he ignored me. Princess was standing by the door looking and grinning with her BIG BUCK TEETH!

***

One day Mua called and told Mom, "It would be a good idea for you to relocate to California. It would give you a chance to get your life together."

Although Mom originally declined, within a few weeks, she changed her mind. A few months later, she came to visit and I was happy for her. However, I didn't want to live with her.

After a short stay, Mom had to go back to Ohio to solidify the move with my younger siblings and I in tow. Princess didn't have to go since she had a summer job.

She always got her way.

She wasn't even old enough to work, she was nine months older than me. I even speculated what Mom did because she had been engaged in adult activity for quite some time. Needless to say, she got a job and I was forced to go with Mom, to look after my younger siblings. (Rolling my eyes)

Mom had three toddlers: Precious, Martina and Pear. Each of them was still sucking the bottle and Pear was wearing pampers and teething. I soon dreaded the long bus ride because I would have to take them to the bathroom, change pampers and sit and watch them while Mom spent most of her time in the back of the bus smoking.

After the long, awful bus ride, when we arrived, Uncle Midnight was there waiting for us. Once we got in the car it was obvious everyone was tired. No one said a word and before long someone began to snore. I looked over to see that both my sisters were asleep and Mom and Uncle Midnight began smoking cigarettes. The smell began to bother me as the wind would blow it in my face and eyes. I held my breath and closed my eyes to block it out and fell asleep.

As we pulled into the parking space, I woke up Precious and Martina. Once inside the house I put them in the bed and went to my bedroom before going to sleep.

A few hours later as I woke up to go to the bathroom, I could hear Mom talking. Not sure who she was talking to, I looked out the window to see Uncle Midnight's car. Trying to hear what was going on, I went downstairs.

It was apparent that Mom was making provision to move. She had gone to get boxes and all the pictures were off the wall. The next morning, she enrolled me and Precious back in my old school. It was good seeing my friends.

***

It didn't take long before Mom was back to her old ways of neglecting her parental duties. It was my responsibility to get myself and Precious to and from school although there were four older brothers at home.

One day Mom didn't come home, and I overslept. With just enough time to get myself to school, I hurried as I quietly got dressed and left.

Later that day, my friends and I walked home from school. As I approached the house, I could see smoke coming through the screen. That was a sign that Mom had returned. As I opened the door, she was standing there smoking a cigarette. The look on her face spoke volumes.

I nervously said, "Hello Mom."

She never acknowledged my presence. I started up the stairs when she blurted out, "Why you didn't take

Precious to school?"

I explained, "I woke up late and only had time to get myself ready," realizing no matter what I said it was going to be a problem.

Now this was a bit much and I never understood her logic. She basically told me that it was hog wash and if I don't have time to get her ready, I can't go.

The next day at school while in class, I was called to the front office. As I approached the door, I saw Precious and she was sitting looking terrified and crying. I was told I had to walk Precious home and I never asked any questions.

On our way home, Precious said she had been standing outside her classroom waiting for Mom. However, Mom never came. As we hurried to get home, I began thinking, "What has happened now?"

When we got home, Mom was sitting on the chair, watching her soaps smoking and drinking. I looked over at her feeling annoyed. I said goodbye and headed back to school. I had walked that distance for many years, however that day it appeared extremely far. I was livid.

Needless to say, this became my daily routine. I would have to miss some class time to take Precious home and walk back to school by myself.

On my way back to school, the traffic guard would be gone. I tried talking to Mom about my own safety, asking her who would walk *me* back to school. From the look on her face, she was bothered, but never changed her mind. I even suggested that she walk and meet us. Now that got me cussed out! She implied that I was being a sassy smart A**.

"Life is no mistake."

TeOnna "TeeTee" Cail

***

The last day of school finally arrived and I was looking forward to my promotion ceremony. That evening, Mom said she had too much work to do in preparation for the move so she would not be able to attend, knowing it was impossible for my father to attend.

I got dressed and walked to the school with some friends and their parents. Even Though I felt sad seeing everyone with their mom. It was normal that my mom never attended an event with me. There were times when she said she despised me.

"Despise is a strong dislike, unworthy of one's notice or consideration."

It was evident by the way she treated me that she didn't value our relationship. She failed to show any interest or curiosity in me or my life.

"People have a different agenda for the relationship than you and they never seek you or your opinion out. Ignore the impact their actions have on you."

I sat there in total awe, taking in every moment. The ceremony was beautiful. I couldn't believe Mom didn't attend and I had never felt so alone.

There were a lot of family members with roses and balloons. As I surveyed the room, almost every girl had a rose except me. Some of their fathers even came.

Imagine my face.

Seeing a room full of distinguished men was breathtaking and the love was epic. It was a bittersweet moment. I thought about the fact that this was the last time I would see my friends because in a few days we would be heading back to California.

At the end of the ceremony, everyone stood around socializing. Not wanting to draw attention to myself I stood there quietly. Although I had to go to the restroom, I refused. I just wanted to crawl back into my skin and die.

Afterwards, a friend had to go to the restroom, so I went as well. During that brief moment, I was able to regain my composure. I was in disbelief that Mom didn't attend and crying wishing my father cared. Knowing I could not look to them for validation or allow what they viewed as a MISTAKE to derail me. They both were the root of the problem and will have to deal with their own demons.

Message To My Father:

Why did you deny Me?

Why did you leave ME?

Why did you hold me and smile in my face?

TONYA "KANDIE" THOMAS

Why didn't I understand?

***

After a brief stay, we were on the bus heading back to California. On the way back, I met a family: a single mom with three exuberant sons and a baby daughter who was cute as a button. They were coming from Alabama.

A few days later, 'mysterious child' and I went over to Donner School to play tetherball. There were several kids already there playing basketball. As we got closer, I noticed it was the boys from the bus.

The oldest boy Leon Jordan was crushing on 'mysterious child.' They lived across the street from the school; what were the chances of that?

We called him 'Big Lee' because he was cool and didn't have any skills. Mama Drew (RIP) had a distinctive voice and feisty demeanor. She would sit on the front porch and watch them as they played.

***

The first day of school was a few days away and I was looking forward to attending Tahoe Elementary School. 'Mysterious child' and I would walk to the bus stop together and I was excited to ride the school bus with my friends Big Lee, Beverly Eaton, and Theresa Giles.

The California school system was different than what I was used to. They had early and late classes. I was accustomed to everyone arriving and being dismissed at the same time; I was in the early class.

Mysterious child's father always sent her money, so Mua would give her an allowance. We would stop at Luckey's to get candy which was unheard of in our house. Her favorites were Lemon Heads and Now N Laters and she would share them with me.

While we waited on the bus, everyone would be playing. There was a large group of boys who were pencil fighting or playing rock paper scissors; these were both new games to me. Not many girls played pencil fights and I never understood rock paper scissors.

I enjoyed my new school where I played on the basketball team. 'Mysterious' was always getting into mischief and she would leave school to go to the store across the street. She was known to be defiant.

Princess was in junior high school and I was glad to be away from her. Being away from her was refreshing.

Fast forward to the next three years at the peak of puberty with raging hormones and everyone was looking for love. Some girls were having babies, running away from home, being promiscuous, involved in prostitution and drugs.

I attended Peter Lassen Junior High School where I met Sondra Roberson, Kerrie Griffin, Jacqueline Junious and Jim Jim (RIP). Jim Jim was Big Lee's God brother.

Princess and Blaze had gotten kicked out and had to go to Leland Stanford, a school for at risk kids. I was glad that I was not living in her shadow.

"Never water down your MISTAKES.

Failures keep you deep rooted in reality.

This will make you strong."

— *Lisa Butler*

***

At this point, I could not stand her. Princess had

reverted to Mom's promiscuous ways. She was a negative influence and a poor example of a big sister. She was on her second pregnancy at fifteen years old.

That's cute.

Mom and my siblings treated her like royalty, catering to her needs. She would sit there big and pregnant with her barf can and instigate because she couldn't do this or that. I felt like they rewarded her for her unmannerly behavior.

Because of her condition, I was responsible for her chores. I asked Mom why I was the only one doing chores and it was the same scenario, different day. She lashed out at me saying, "Do what I tell you and don't worry about anyone else. Princess has enough with her being pregnant and boys don't do dishes that's how punks are made!"

Mom's reasons and lies were becoming more irritating. I could see right through her crap and I knew it was going to be no more throwing shade from Princess. She had been pushing my buttons for years. I never saw her fight, and although she was bigger than me, I had been sizing her up for quite some time. I was confident that she didn't stand a chance and I was ready to unleash on her. I thought to myself, "After she has her baby it's on!"

Time to put up or shut up.

Fast Forward… Princess gave birth to a healthy baby boy who was a ball of joy.

I was looking forward to summer break. Because Princess had a summer job, I was forced to babysit. Although I didn't want to, I had no other choice.

I made the best of it; my bestie Beverly's sister had a baby boy also. We would take the boys for strolls to the park.

Several months later, Princess' new boyfriend was visiting and she was showing out. As I attempted to ignore her, her aggressive tone and nasty attitude fueled my anger. Moreso, I always knew her bark was bigger than her bite.

Before I knew it, I was making good on my promise. I had her in a head lock, banging her head against the wall and heater. All while she is tried to pick up her son to deflect.

Her boyfriend was in disbelief. She heard about me and knew I was no joke with my hands. When I realized what she was trying to do I snatched her with all my might. The loud noise alarmed Mua because the walls were thin.

Mua lived next door, but. she came bursting in the door. I never acknowledged her presence. When I was done, the silence spoke volumes.

No one ever asked any questions.

This brought a different form of respect for Kandie!

After the beat down, I was labeled crazy for lack of a better term. People would ask her about me and she always had something negative to say, "....You know she is crazy."

Hey! LOL ... I will take that if that's the best you can say.

Now that everyone knew it was not going to be any more jokes at my expense. There was a major shift in the way they looked at me. I knew it was in her best interest to stay in her place because I was at my wits ends. Although I was resolute in how I was going to move forward, I was not going to continue to subject myself to this negative environment. More so, it was not conducive to the woman I desired to be.

Having to live in the shadows of my parents' misconduct was a hindrance and I did not want to be another statistic for teenage pregnancy.

I thought this would encourage Mom to redeem herself.

I asked her to put me on birth control. After a good

cussing out, she said, "Ain't no more babies coming in my damn house."

I stood there thinking, "Why are you so cold and callous towards me? At least I had the decency to ask since you never initiated the conversation."

It was hard to stay focused being a motherless child and a daddyless daughter. I was crying so hard on the inside I was drowning in my tears as my heart was fluttering. I was coming to grips with the reality that my mom didn't want or love me, Mr. Husband had to move forward with his life and my father died leaving me in limbo. Being victimized by my parents for many years left me broken.

Message To My Father:

I understand you were a man.

I understand you had no plans.

I understand it was out of your hands.

MISTAKES ARE MADE FOR *a reason*

I understand God had other plans.

Although you never spoke a word.

Your presence spoke volumes.

***

Laura Gleghorn-Keene Appling was always a ray of sunshine and she always had a word of encouragement. She taught me how to braid extensions and paid me to do her hair. For my sixteenth birthday, she gave me gold chain with a 'Sweet 16' charm on it. The love she showed was the highlight of my day.

One day, Beverly Eaton, Karen Keene, Cassaundra Willis, Cherie Spooner, and I went to Fourth Avenue Park aka Pebble Beach. We played basketball and hung out. Beverly and I always liked a good game of hoop and we were competitive when it came to basketball.

TONYA "KANDIE" THOMAS

Judy Chouteau and her sister Tanya Jackson were sitting on the grass. Not long afterwards, a group of guys came to play. They needed both courts so we sat and watched. I met Eddie who had moved from Phoenix, Arizona.

When I got home, Mom had passed out and the house was normal. There were a million different things going on. I went to my bedroom and sat alone in deep thought.

Days later, he and his cousin came over to my house uninvited. I almost lost it on them. He saw the look of discontent on my face and politely left.

Everything that was going on was mind blowing. The next time I saw Eddie, I told him that was not the business. In fear of Mom unleashing on me. He understood and respected my decision.

He was a few years older. Shortly afterwards, we were vibing. He had good energy.

" Do the best you can until you know better. Then when you know better, do better."

—Maya Angelou

TONYA "KANDIE" THOMAS

CHAPTER 7:

Rage

I buried my head in my pillow crying, thinking about how my presence had a negative impact on their ideal family. All the pieces of the puzzle were complete.

Realizing it was not a dream or a MISTAKE it was my dark reality. Mr. Husband was not my biological father, but he was the only father figure in my life. My life was a constant reminder of how my father never uttered a word of value and how Mom was always spiteful, and Princess made it clear every chance she got with my siblings validating her actions. They were like that and it irked my nerves to realize they were addicted to negativity.

The daughterly love I had from them had dwindled to ashes and dissipated into the thin air. From the way Mom looked, talked, walked and how she blew that nasty cigarette smoke through her nostrils. She was not open to talking and obviously didn't care about the outcome.

My father had no emotional connection and I refused

to be bound by what they viewed as a 'mistake.' I realized I had been victimized for far too long.

I saw him a few times prior to his untimely death. During our spontaneous visits, the look of admiration that he displayed spoke volumes. Moreso, how in the HELL do you visit with your innocent daughter and never utter a word or man up to your responsibilities?

An introduction would have been nice.

As the tears began welling up in my eyes, dropping rapidly, I knew I could not give in. Although Their deceitful conduct enraged me as my mind went from one extreme to another.

CASE AND POINT:

As a woman and mother, I would have never allowed a man to treat me in such a despicable manner. I am appalled by my parents' deceitful scandalous behavior. I would never give a man control over my mind or my body. I would never allow him to deny my child. I would never allow him to use sex as a weapon. I would never allow him to make me feel lesser than a woman. Having experienced disrespect from both parents has been heart wrenching!

Whenever I expressed my feelings about the effect Mom's behavior was causing, my siblings acted like I created the problems and I was making a big issue out of nothing; they always had each other's back. They would justify her ignorance by saying, "Well that's Mom."

"THATS CUTE." Nope!!

As Mom continued resuming her old ways, this perturbed me to no end.

***

She was dating a self-proclaimed atheist and a known alcoholic. The fact that he was an alcoholic didn't surprise me since that   was   the   common denominator. ALCOHOL is one thing, but Satan! Make that make sense!

Mom allowed Satan to move in.

He was very disrespectful. He would walk around the house in his boxers, cussing like a mad sailor. It bothered me that he had little to no respect for us or Mom.

This was very much out of the norm. I have never seen any of my five brothers do that. When I would say something about it Mom would say, "Turn your damn head."

Apparently, she didn't see anything wrong with it. I realized our relationship was in dire crisis and beyond repair and I desired to tell Mua or anyone who cared.

He spoke about being an atheist with the intent of trying to derail my beliefs. Not wanting to continue to live like that, I wanted to remove myself at all costs.

I began to examine the situation as I had often done. Each time, I got the same revelation: I felt STUCK!

Realizing that they can't give me what they don't have and I refused to succumb to my negative environment and live in fear of the unknown. To make matters worse, I had to cook and clean for Satan.

I thank God I am not a creature of habit or have a submissive, addictive personality. I could not continue to be quiet, I had to demand respect.

Not long after, I considered an escape plan. Thinking about the army would be a way of escape. Of course, Mom had negative comments and had a darn fit and belittled me. I was taken aback as I stood there and listened to this angry black woman assassinate my character and devalue my worth. She said, "You want to come back liking women."

I looked at her in disbelief. She continued making derogatory comments. I stood thinking this is as barbaric as it gets. I wanted to say I am looking for love and a way out.

Later that day, I was at my breaking point. It was evident that their contagious, barbaric spirit had affected me. Feeling defeated, I walked to the end of the block at the corner of 44th street and 10th avenue. I linked up with Shelli Car'mel and Gai Toi Williams and shared my feelings. I told them I hated my mom and wanted to kill myself. They never asked why and I never spoke about it again.

I was overwhelmed with pain & the shame was too much to share. We had been friends for a few years and Shelli's sisters were good friends with Princess. We laughed and as she said, "Sometimes my mom and sisters get on my nerves, but I don't want to kill myself."

She gave me the biggest hug as we all leaped into the

air and exhaled laughing. As we continued our way, I recall thinking what she said made a lot of sense.

When we got to the park, it was good to see Bernard Hodge. Everyone was excited about the new park. Once it started to get dark, we all headed home. On my way home, I remember feeling like crap and disgusted with the unjust treatment I had to deal with. I was thinking, "What was the big deal about my father? What is the big secret?"

A few days later, my cousin's younger sister and I were walking to the park. I saw a girl who approached me being hostile. Not liking conflict, I turned to walk away. She then attempted to charge me. Needless to say, we held up traffic on a busy street. And the rest is HIS-TORY!

***

A few weeks later, I got in a fight after school with a girl from a rival school. I didn't know her and had never seen her. I was at basketball practice and she was doing hand gestures trying to get my attention. I am one who doesn't argue so I attempted to de-escalate the situation by ignoring her and walking away.

By the time I exited the school grounds there was a large crowd gathered at the end of the street. She was waiting with a group of friends. As I walked towards the crowd, I could hear her talking crap, which made my adrenaline rush.

When I reached the designated spot, I hit her with all my power. She hit the ground and I got on top of her and started banging her head on the concrete ground.

I was full of rage.

Shortly afterwards, I could see blood. Once I heard the sirens of the ambulance and police I got scared. Everyone began screaming, "Get up Kandie the police are coming."

I jumped up and got on the back of DJ's bike. When

he got me far away from the crime scene, I walked home. Later that day, we met at Jack Davis Park. And I was told she had a concussion. I felt bad, but she brought it on herself.

The next day on the way to school, that was the highlight of our conversation. Everyone told me that I was a beast and how I beat her butt. As I walked in the building there were several policemen. They approached me and took me into the principal's office for interrogation and called my mom.

After the intense questioning, there were no repercussions on my part. I was defending myself since she had skipped school to come to fight me, although she was in the hospital with a concussion.

Boy, was I relieved.

I was given a pass to go to class. Later that day when I got home, Mom asked me, "Why didn't you tell me about the fight?"

I nervously said, "I didn't know."

After a few choices of words, I walked away. I was not going to stand there and listen as she belittled me. It was obvious the principal told her it was not my fault.

As I entered the bedroom, Princess was sitting on her bed with her son because he was sick with colic. He would cry all the time, mostly at night and I was to blame for him getting sick.

Mua was alarmed by his cries and gave him some medicine. The first few nights, he cried nonstop. Mom's boyfriend said some unpleasant things and Mom didn't check the situation. Princess cussed him out and Mom tried to defend him; then Princess cussed *her* out.

I stood there looking in disbelief, waiting for Mom to address the issue; she never did. She went into her room, closed the door and Princess continued to talk. She was mad at Mom and was trying to get me to engage in conversation with her. Although Mom was wrong, I didn't voice my opinion. It felt good seeing them at each other's throats for once and I was not part of the problem.

The next few days, you could feel the heaviness in the house. The medicine was beginning to work and my nephew was crying less and sleeping more. My siblings were at odds with Mom regarding the situation. They asked me what happened, so I lied and told them I wasn't sure and I didn't hear what was said.

Princess was angry that I didn't have her back. As I laughed on the inside, I thought, "Now *you* know how it feels."

Even though I wanted to come to her aid, I couldn't. It was hard allowing Mom to think I was defending her actions. Once I realized Mom thought I was on her side I completely removed myself.

"Think about a time you bought something and never used it, consider how you handled it..."

— Tonya "Kandie" Thomas

I didn't intend to continue living like this, feeling unloved, unwanted, and just taking up space.

One day as Mom and I were sitting in the living room, we heard the mailman. Mom opened the door to retrieve the mail. As she fumbled through the mail, she separated the junk mail.

After seeing several coupons and sale ads there was a white bulk envelope that got her immediate attention. She placed all the other mail on the bar and went to the bathroom. She stayed there for an extended time then she exited. She walked right past me and made a beeline out the front door, passed

Mua's house and straight across the street in full stride to her friend's house.

Within a few minutes, I could hear her talking loudly. I looked out the door to see her standing there waving the papers which explained the nature of her frustration.

Not knowing what was going on, I turned off the television and went next door. As I sat on the porch and tentatively listened, Mom repeated several times, "His witness lied! They need to leave me alone and mind their own business."

As I sat there puzzled trying to figure out what was going on…. **His** WITNESS! What they said and why Mom was upset. I knew all the information was in the letter. I kept thinking, "What did the letter say? Who was the witness?"

Not knowing what was going on, I sat quietly listening as she continued to rant. She never took ownership in what was being said and was cautious not to incriminate herself. Shortly afterwards, Mom came walking back across the street as I sat there watching her walk home looking like a deer in headlights clutching the letter. Her heart was beating as fast as she was walking. The closer she got to me the bigger her eyes got.

Although she never looked at me, I glanced at her through my peripheral vision as she walked by and I could feel a breeze of hot air, witnessing the look of defeat. After sitting there for a while not knowing what to do, I went to check on mom.

I quietly entered the house and tipped toed towards her bedroom. As I got closer, I could hear her snoring & whimpering. Now I was even more concerned because the whimpering was intense, like a deep gut-wrenching sound.

As I stood there feeling helpless, I noticed the envelope and letter sitting on top of the television. Not knowing what to do, I felt stuck between a rock and a hard place. I figured that this may be my only opportunity since no one else was home to read the letter.

Although I was apprehensive, seeing Mom like that was heartbreaking. My curiosity got the best of me. I took the letter in the bathroom and began reading it.

It was a resolution of marriage. Mr. Husband had filed for a divorce and aired the ugly truth. It detailed pertinent information regarding their irreconcilable differences. He named their children and I was not included. Although Aunt Pony told me years ago when she took us shopping, reading it was mind blowing.

Now that was a TKO!

The house was still eerily quiet. I could still hear Mom snoring and whimpering. I hurried out of the bathroom and placed the envelope back where I got it from. I ran over to Basil's house displaying the same pain that Mom was exhibiting. Explaining what

I read knocked the wind out of me. It was a dagger in the heart and I was devastated.

I was not upset that Mr. Husband took legal action and exposed her, but I was livid about how I had to find out and I felt devalued.

"Devaluing is anything that diminishes or destroys the personhood of the other. Treating the other person as if they are not deserving of honor, empathy, love, compassion, and respect as a child of God. Never allow someone or thing to make you feel less of a person.

Later that day, Mom's cousin and his friends came over during their lunch break. I sat there waiting to hear if she was going to disclose the details but she never did. She told them about being served divorce papers. Seeing her clavier reactions, I sat there waiting to hear if she was going to disclose the details. Mom spoke about the witnesses lying on her without stating what was said. After all, it was difficult for Mom to own her mess. They stated that she was an unfit mother and she sent her three minor daughters to live with her mother in Sacramento, California.

I was hoping she would acknowledge her shortcomings.

"Your lies will only carry you so far. Once they run their course, the real you is still there looking for a way out of the hole you dug for yourself."

—Tonya "Kandie" Thomas

I wanted to ask Mom why she was acting so surprised. I want to reiterate what Aunt Pony said and tell her I read the letter. Due to fear, I never did.

"Fear is false evidence appearing real."

I was at my breaking point and fear dissipated. I realized it was false evidence appearing real. I intentionally got pregnant and not because I flunked sex education. I was seeking love and a way out. The stress led to a very difficult pregnancy.

***

Eddie was forced to move back to his hometown Phoenix, Arizona. He reassured me that he would take care of me and our unborn child. While sitting on the porch Mua suggested that I was pregnant. She told me that she dreamed of fish and that meant someone was pregnant. She suggested I tell Mom. Although I was scared, I knew I had to face the giant.

Once I told Mom, it went from bad to worse. Early in my second trimester I was put on bed rest due to complications. As I was lying in bed resting, looking forward to having a healthy baby, I followed the doctor's orders. Mom told me to walk to the store. I reminded her of my high-risk pregnancy and the doctor's orders...

I was on bed rest.

She wasn't trying to hear what I was saying. As we headed out the door towards Stockton Boulevard, I was even more agitated watching her smoke a cigarette. She didn't say much.

As we got closer to the store, I saw her boyfriend's car parked on the corner of 6th avenue and Stockton Boulevard. Now I am *really* mad.

Once we got to the store, Mom made a beeline to the bar next door. When we walked in, she saw him and slapped him on the back of his head. As everyone began watching, Mom pulled out the bar stool and sat at the bar next to him like nothing happened.

MISTAKES ARE MADE FOR *a reason*

***

Early one spring morning, I was awakened. I went to the bathroom several times. I was not able to go back to sleep, so I laid there in bed. With my due date fast approaching, the thought of becoming a mother was surreal.

As I laid there, the discomfort became intense. Not knowing what to do, I realized that I was having contractions. I knocked on Mom's bedroom door and she began yelling and cussing about me waking her up. I saw her light was on and heard them talking.

I then went into my bedroom and knocked on the wall as hard as I could. To get Mua's attention. She came running over and called the ambulance. Mua told Mom to get dressed so she could ride with me. She had every excuse in the book and I was not surprised.

I was hoping she would be quiet, not to mention I didn't want her negative energy. I was tired of hearing her complaints and her hardened heart had vexed my spirit.

I grabbed my bag as we waited.

Once the paramedic arrived after a few questions they strapped me on the gurney. Mua told me to call her to let her know how I was doing and off we went.

As I was being transported. I was crying and feeling lonely. It was horrible having to hear Mom's cruel comments as I remained respectful. I thought she never showed any compassion towards me. I was in pain and didn't need this stress.

She never acknowledged it and continued to antagonize me. The medic checked me and told me I was fully dilated and my blood pressure was a little high. Not wanting to have any complications I began to pull it together. He retook my blood pressure once again before we arrived at the hospital and it was much better.

While I was being prepped for delivery, Uncle Smooth and Mom came into my room. It made me feel good that they came, however I was hoping she would come with a better attitude. She came on the same bull crap.

I felt my blood pressure skyrocket and minutes later she said, "We will be back, I am going to smoke a cigarette."

I was glad to see her go. I saw her about two hours later when I was in recovery. I had given birth to a healthy feisty baby girl. She was a ball of joy weighing four pounds and eleven ounces.

Mom stood next to my bed telling me how worthless I was and it was not in my best interest to spoil her because ain't no crying a** baby going to be keeping her man up all night. I looked over at her trying to make it make sense.

She left and I was happy to see her go. The next few

days were an eye opener. I used that time to rest and get my thoughts in order.

"Mistakes are inevitable; they will propel or derail you."

— Tonya "Kandie" Thomas

***

I felt hopeless realizing a baby was a big responsibility and I had not thought it through. However, there was no looking back.

After Mom scrutinized me about thinking about going to the army and declined to allow me to take birth control. I intentionally got pregnant as a means of escape. The desire to be loved propelled me to have a baby with the hope it would be reciprocated.

Having a baby was an indescribable feeling. Considering my age and situation, my mind went from one extreme to another. As I glanced out the window from my hospital room, I thought about what Mom said.

I could not understand her reasoning so I began to cry. I was overwhelmed with the thought of not knowing what to expect and I was a ball of emotions.

As the tears began to flow, the uncertainty illuminated my mind. My child and I could be homeless if she cried one too many times. These thoughts made my life flash before me; my mind was fixated on everything my parents had done and anger surged through me.

She was always intentional. I had accepted the fact that Mom had viewed me as a mistake and obliterated me. As the tears were streaming down my face, I was lying there wrestling with the statement Mom made earlier. At that moment I realized Mom always had an ill intent.

I was not even sure why I was shocked. Although I couldn't get the statement out of my mind, the thought of being a mother brought me joy.

The nurse came in to check on me. As she checked my vitals, I tried to hide the tears. She told me my blood pressure was high and asked me how my pain was.

I never responded.

Seeing that I was an emotional wreck, she then showed me a chart exemplifying my pain level with the numbers of one through ten; one being the least and ten being the most.

Unable to control the tears I pointed to ten. She told me my blood pressure was high and would let the doctor know. Once she was finished she left and reassured she would be back with pain medicine to manage my pain.

I thought, "No medicine is going to help the pain I

have been experiencing."

She assumed my pain was physical and I went with it. When she returned, she said the doctor requested that I take a stronger dosage to relieve the pain, calm my nerves and lower my blood pressure.

After taking the medicine, I drifted off to a deep peaceful sleep. It was the best sleep I had had in a long time. I got up and went to the nursery to see my daughter. She was sleeping as I stood there admiring her.

The doctor walked over to me as we began chatting. He explained, "She's lost two pounds and I'm concerned. She may have to stay in the hospital once you are discharged."

That hit me like a ton of bricks.

But the joy of her gave me the strength to push forward and my maternal instinct kicked in. I acknowledged I allowed them to annihilate me. I owned my part. However, I was not going to allow my child to be subjected to the abuse. The fact that I am her mother, it was my job to provide and protect my daughter at all costs.

Six weeks later, I went to the doctor for my well woman check-up and I was medically cleared. The next day I asked Mom if I could go to Phoenix to visit Eddie for a few weeks. To God be glory she said 'yes.' For the first time in my life, she agreed with me.

IMAGINE THAT!!

I was overjoyed as I began packing quietly. I was praying she didn't change her mind and praying Princess cleared it. I called Eddie and told him Mom said yes. I requested he send us a one-way bus ticket.

Basil and his friend took us to the Greyhound Bus Station. When it was time to board the bus, I began feeling uneasy. I was nervous, excited, and eager.

Although I had traveled cross country by bus several times. This time was very different.

My baby girl and I were in pursuit of happiness and love. Once the bus departed, the joy I felt was unexplainable and it took a moment to gather my thoughts. With a resilient spirit and a fearful heart, it was hard to contain my emotions.

My heart was racing and my body was numb. The sense of fear was evident in my reactions. The decisions I had made in the past were an eye opener. The palpation from my heart and the tingling in my hands and feet were intense.

Not knowing what to expect, I felt apprehensive traveling to an unfamiliar place. Despite being excited that Mom obliged and was eager to embrace what God has in store for us, I was coming to grips with my decision.

I allowed myself to be victimized at the hands of my parents for far too long and this robbed me of my childhood. I spent my whole life pretending to be happy, pressing through the pain, shame and grief that had taken residence in my life; this was difficult.

The desire to satisfy my emotional need was to be loved and they couldn't give me what they did not have. Everyone wants to be loved and I committed to remain true to my daughter and myself and not to mimic my parents' behavior.

"Love is being true to oneself. When people show you who you are, believe them."

As the sun set, I looked over at my beautiful daughter and began to realize failure was not an option and it was an honor and a privilege to be her mother. Before long I engulfed the moment and my mind began shifting. I prayed to God to keep us safe.

As I looked over at my baby, she was sleeping peacefully. I took her out of her carrier and held her tight to profess my love. I whispered In her ear as I looked in her eyes and said, "I promise to provide & protect you at all costs. My love is as intentional as God and His unchanging hands."

I then asked God to continue to shield us of any hurt, harm & danger and that He would elevate us to higher heights as He enlarged our territory. Shortly afterwards I drifted off to sleep and early the next day we arrived in Phoenix, Arizona.

***

As the bus pulled into the depot I stood up and stretched my arms, thanking God for traveling mercy and a safe journey. Once I gathered our stuff, WE exited the bus with our dignity.

"NOT ANGER. NOT MAD. JUST DONE!"

"And they overcame him by the blood of the lamb and by the word of their testimony."

~Revelation 12:11 (KJV)

Prior to writing this book, I was so numb with pain that you could have pinched me, and I would not have felt it. My greatest fear was to die of a broken heart.

Although it has been liberating, writing this book has been by far the hardest challenge I have faced. It was difficult reliving those horrific moments. However, with an obedient spirit and an open mind I followed the guidance of the Holy Spirit, which increased my faith.

After many distractions and life altering events, God arrested, empowered, and equipped me. My prayer is that my testimony inspires anyone in need of love and more so at-risk teen girls. I want you to know that *you matter!*

It's not a MISTAKE you are reading my book. It's by divine intention to activate your faith and empower you. If you have faith as a mustard seed, you have power.

I have always desired to share my story with hopes of rescuing someone in need. Through all my adversities, life has been the best teacher. I have learned humility, compassion, and resilience.

Sharing my story has been therapeutic and has given me the closure I desperately yearned for.

Before I formed you in the womb, I knew you. Before you were born, I set you apart; I appointed you as a prophet to the nations.
~Jeremiah 1:5 (NIV)

TONYA "KANDIE" THOMAS

Tonya "Kandie" Thomas

THROUGH THE YEARS

REFERENCES:

- Youngstown, Ohio history

(Best Places) **https://www.bestplaces.net**

(Travel lens) **https://www.travellens.com**

- Signs of a controlling relationship:
  https://www.raw.org.au
- Love vs control **https://www.needhelp.ca**
- Crib death **https://www.cancer.gov** NCI
  Dictionary of cancer terms
- Without coordination
  https://www.marriagetrac.com
- The keys to a successful Marriage-Health
  Encyclopedia -URMC Marriage takes work
  hptts://www.urmc.rochester.edu>c
- **Respecting each other:**
  Https://www.lovingatyourbest.com

- The Roles of a mother

  https://www.continue.com

- Emotional Healing Facebook **https://Ms-my.Facebook.com**

- Entanglement Cambridge Dictionary **https://dictionary.Cambridge**

- Irish twins Peanut App:

  https:www.mamanatural.com

- Serenity Prayer

  hptts://www.cincinnatichildrens.org

- Serenity Oxford Dictionary

  https://en.m.Wikipedia.org

- Denial

  https://www.verywellmind.com

  Https://www.Betterhelp.com

- Anxiety

  o   Oxford Dictionary

  o   Wits end Cambridge Dictionary

  o   Obliterate Cambridge Dictionary

- Https://dictionary.Cambridge.org
- Carefree

  Cambridge Dictionary

A father Oxford Dictionary

- A mother's love: **https:wwwinterflora.in>blog**
- Adultery: **https://www.law.Cornell.edu>wex**
- Devaluing: **https://we.btr.org**
- Kindergarten:

  https://www.alpinemontessori.com
- Hate: **https://www.everydayhealth.com**
- Denial: **https://www.dictionary.com**
- Jealousy: **https://wwwpsychologytoday.com**
- Despise Merriam -Webster
- Signs someone may not care:

  https://psychocentral.com> blog > h
- Abortion: Oxford Dictionary
- Anxiety: Oxford Dictionary
- Bewildered: Oxford Dictionary
- Diva: **https:/www.urbandictionary.com**

TONYA "KANDIE" THOMAS

ABOUT THE AUTHOR

Tonya Kandie Thomas

Tonya "Kandie" Thomas was born and raised in Youngstown, Ohio, but relocated to Sacramento, California at a young age. She graduated from the Sacramento public school system.

She accepted the Lord Jesus Christ as her savior at the tender age of nine years old. Living with her grandmother afforded her a closer relationship with

God and strengthened her faith. She is the sixth of ten children. Her parents were married but not to one another and she was conceived from their adulterous affair. She was viewed as a **MISTAKE,** which caused her a tremendous amount of shame and pain. This is where the book, *'Mistakes Are Made For A Reason'* was born.

The lack of love from her parents and being ostracized by her siblings derailed her. For many years, she wrestled with rejection, rage, abandonment, and suicidal tendencies. The desire to be loved thrust her into early adulthood/ motherhood at the tender age of seventeen years old.

After giving birth to her daughter, she relocated to Phoenix Arizona.

When Tonya began her new life, it was always her desire to share her story. She registered for the Celebrate Recovery Program, which is a twelve-step program designed to change her life. This program helped her to receive the breakthrough she needed, giving her the courage to write her book.

Tonya is a Celebrate Recovery Facilitator and participated in grief counseling to help her cope with loss.

She is a motivational speaker and serial author who desires to minister to at risk teen girls. It is her hope that her story will encourage and inspire someone who believes their life isn't worth living.

She is the mother of two beautiful daughters and six grandchildren, and resides in Avondale, Arizona.

TONYA "KANDIE" THOMAS

MISTAKES ARE MADE FOR *a reason*

CONTACT THE AUTHOR

You can find Tonya online by
visiting her website:

WWW.TonyaThomas.Com

To book Tonya for your next event:

 T.BeBless@yahoo.com

You can follow Tonya on social
media:

@TonyaKandieThomas

TONYA "KANDIE" THOMAS

Made in the USA
Las Vegas, NV
22 June 2023

73724622R00133